Brilliant Manager

Brilliant Manager

What the best managers know, do and say

Nic Peeling

Harlow, England • London • New York • Boston • San Francisco • Toronto • Sydney • Tokyo • Singapore • Hong Kong
Seoul • Taipei • New Delhi • Cape Town • Madrid • Mexico City • Amsterdam • Munich • Paris • Milan

PEARSON EDUCATION LIMITED

Edinburgh Gate
Harlow CM20 2JE
Tel: +44 (0)1279 623623
Fax: +44 (0)1279 431059
Website: www.pearsoned.co.uk

First published in Great Britain in 2005

ISBN 0 273 70213 0

British Library Cataloguing-in-Publication Data
A catalogue record for this book is available from the British Library

Library of Congress Cataloging-in-Publication Data
Peeling, Nic.
Brilliant manager : what the best managers know, do and say / Nic Peeling.
p. cm.
Includes bibliographical references and index.
ISBN 0-273-70213-0 (alk. paper)
1. Management—Handbooks, manuals, etc. I. Title.

HD38.15.P44 2005
658—dc22

2005048671

10 9 8 7 6 5 4 3 2 1
09 08 07 06 05

Cartoon illustrations by Bill Piggins
Typeset in 11pt Minion by 70
Printed and bound in Great Britain by Bell & Bain Ltd, Glasgow

The publisher's policy is to use paper manufactured from sustainable forests.

To Sue, Harriet, Jilly, Julie and Sally

Contents

Introduction

There is a very clear distinction between good and bad management. The fact that we all laugh at Dilbert means that we all have the same idea about what bad management is. Perhaps more surprisingly, anybody lucky enough to work for a brilliant manager will probably find that all the rest of the team have an equally good opinion of their boss. Generally, it's easy to see good and bad management in other people. However, it's far less easy to see it in yourself, and harder still to know what it is that you need to change to become a brilliant manager.

What is it that brilliant managers know, do and say that makes them so good at their jobs? If you want to know … read on. The good news is that most brilliant managers use a very similar set of core techniques – this book will show you what they are, and how to adopt them for yourself.

Brilliant Manager is for anyone who is a frontline manager, dealing directly with staff, customers, senior management and the like. It is the first book to try to distil the hard-won experience of the best managers and set it down as practical things you need to know, do and say.

The sections covered are:

Managing people – Very few managers receive training in managing difficult staff issues. Making the wrong decision could cause someone real pain. This thought should scare you. How do you make sure you handle every situation the right way?

Leadership – You are not just a manager: your team is looking to you for answers, for direction, for inspiration – and you thought managing people was scary! What do you need to do to be seen as a leader as well as a manager?

Culture – Some teams have great team spirit and obviously share the same values and aspirations. How do you foster a strong team culture?

Managing different types of people – Different professions (lawyers, IT staff, salesmen, consultants) all bring their own problems, as do creative staff and support staff. How do you best manage these different types of people?

Organizing your team – As a team grows in size, the pressures on you will build up. How do you manage these pressures using tried and tested techniques?

Business management – Even if you do not have specific financial responsibility for profit and loss, your job is to focus the delivery of your team's products and services, and to market them to your customers. What are the principles of good business management that you can apply to your team's business?

Managing your organization – The better your team delivers results, the more others in your organization will see it as a threat. There will be a constant stream of initiatives from your own organization that seem to be designed to stop your team doing its job. You have to act as the interface between your team and the rest of the organization. Losing your temper is not the way to handle this role – but what is?

Knowing it, doing it, saying it – There is a massive gulf between the theory and practice of management. A number of real-life scenarios will help bridge that gulf.

Literal reading warning

I am assuming you are a busy person. I want you to read this book, so I have kept it short and written in a style that is easy to read. However, there are dangers in the style that I use:

- You may take me too literally. I exaggerate and simplify some points to help them hit home. My aim is to help you think about the issues, not to produce a recipe that can be followed precisely. Every management job has its own unique context, and this book must be interpreted sensibly in the context you work within. For example, if your team is losing lots of money then you will need to adopt a management approach that is appropriate to what is probably a life or death situation – ER doctors do not usually have the time to discuss treatment with their patients!
- I will make issues seem simpler than they really are. You may read parts of this book, think you understand the points being made, and then not know what to do in a real-life situation. I think that the theory of management is simple – it's the practice that's hard and it cannot be learned from a book. What I have tried to do is to provide a framework for you to think about your job and to make lots of suggestions for techniques that you might like to try.

The golden rule of management

Before moving on to the rest of the book I want to start with the single most important rule of management:

> *You will be judged by your actions, not by your words, and your actions set the example for your team to follow.*

The implications of this rule will appear time and again, in numerous different forms, throughout this book.

Your actions set the example for your team to follow

Acknowledgements

I would like to thank my employers QinetiQ for allowing me the use of work facilities to write this book.

I am indebted to Neil Hepworth, who read each chapter as it was first written and gave me such encouragement and sound advice during the creation of this book.

I was most fortunate in having so many friends and colleagues who read the book and gave me feedback on it, including Mark Gamble, Cath Hipwood, Ken and Christine Magowan, Steve Mitchell, Michael O'Mahony, Eric Peeling, Thomas Petford, Jutta Spaniol, Sally and David Rees, Rob Rowlingson, Julian Satchell, Mike Wild, Arthur Williams and Harriet Yeoman. I am particularly indebted to Richard Chisnall, Duncan Machray, Betty Mackman, Matthew Peck, Anne-Marie Rocca and Alan Watson for their line-by-line critiques of early drafts.

I had so many conversations with friends and colleagues about the subject matter of the book that it is impossible to name them all individually; you know who you are and please accept my thanks.

Finally, thanks to the team at Pearson Education and, in particular, to my publisher Rachael Stock for believing so strongly in my book.

CHAPTER 1

Managing people

The thought of writing this chapter was what motivated me to write this book in the first place. Let's face it, the average standard of managing people is far from brilliant, so this is a very good place to start a book about becoming a brilliant manager.

I would like to start with an optimistic observation:

> *People in a work context are very forgiving. If your performance improves then your staff will very soon forget your past lapses.*

This means that you can turn round the team's view of your management style very quickly indeed.

I will also restate the golden rule of management in an appropriate form:

> *The simplest way to get your staff to behave in a particular way is to behave that way yourself.*

Fundamental principles of managing people

One of the problems that managers face when managing people is that they often have not accepted the fact that the principles of people management are very similar to the principles of being a good parent or a good teacher, namely:

- setting high expectations of people's performance and behaviour;
- setting clear boundaries of acceptable behaviour;
- imposing discipline and, where necessary, punishment when behaviour is unacceptable;
- setting clear boundaries of acceptable performance; working with underperforming staff to improve their performance; if performance cannot be improved in your team you must decide if they need to leave your team or, in extremis, whether they need to leave the organization;
- providing clear, immediate feedback on performance and behaviour; praise good performance, and constructively criticize poor performance;
- personally setting an example of the performance and behaviour you expect;
- behaving in a way that wins the respect of your team.

Being a parent or teacher is a great responsibility. Brilliant managers have to accept that they are doing a job with similar levels of responsibility. You may find this uncomfortable as a manager, but your staff will have no trouble at all accepting that this is the way brilliant managers should behave.

Is management manipulation?

I would really like to believe that you can be a manager without being manipulative, but there will be times when a manager has got to be manipulative. The uncomfortable truth is that when resolving all the different pressures from existing customers, your own organization, bids for new business and the like, you are inevitably going to have to persuade people to do things that are not entirely in their own interests.

It is also an uncomfortable truth that you are not always going to be in a position where you can explain the bigger picture to all your staff. All that you can hope to achieve is that your manipulation is moral. My definition of moral manipulation would be:

> *If your team knew the whole picture, the majority would support your actions.*

One of the reasons for mentioning the issue of manipulation is that many managers complain that their staff are suspicious of their motives. It basically comes down to whether your staff respect and trust you. Staff suspicion is quite natural and you can only create the necessary levels of trust and respect by your openness, honesty and integrity. This raises a key issue:

How open should you be?

A good starting point is to be as open and honest *as possible.* The problems lie in defining what that nasty get-out clause 'as possible' means in practice. I will tackle this issue by listing the circumstances in which I believe less than total openness is acceptable:

- *When you have to respect confidentiality.* You may be instructed by your organization to keep certain information confidential, or you may not be able to release information that was told to you in confidence.
- *When you have to support 'the corporate line'.* This will be discussed in more detail in a later chapter.
- *When full openness would cause unnecessary pain.* For example, you may be discussing how a member of your team can improve their performance. You may need to be selective about telling the staff member about their failings in order that they can handle – and respond positively to – your criticism.

- *When full disclosure will unnecessarily depress your team.* A good example might be the latest initiatives from head office. Many of these never actually get implemented in a way that is as threatening as they first appear. My approach to such issues is to openly answer any questions about them. I always try to go occasionally to group gatherings, e.g. at coffee time, so that people can quiz me. In this way I make it clear that there is no secret about what is going on, but I also imply that I am relaxed about such things, and that when, or if, they impinge on the team I will immediately brief everyone.
- *When the effort of communication is not worthwhile.* You will never have enough time to communicate with your team as much as you would like. This means you have to prioritize your communication, and consequently some issues will drop off the bottom. The next section discusses this further.

How to organize communications in your team

I will start with two slightly depressing observations. First, no matter how well you manage the communications within your team, it is likely that most of your team members will feel they are not kept properly informed. Second, under the pressures most managers face, the first thing to suffer is usually communications.

I wish I could lay out an easy plan for you to follow, but the best I can do is lay down a few useful guidelines.

*Ensure that matters that **directly** affect staff are discussed with them before irrevocable decisions are taken*

It is a well-known psychological effect that people who feel that they have no control over their environment become anxious, stressed and demotivated. Consequently, the maximum irritation comes from staff finding out that decisions that affect them directly have been taken without any consultation with them. I suggest you make such matters your top communication priority. Remember that you do not have to do all communication personally; you can use other members of your team's organization as appropriate. However, it is good practice to make sure that you give bad news personally.

Make yourself available for informal questions

If your team see that you are not hiding away from their questions, they are much less likely to think you are deliberately keeping things from them.

Keep formal communication meetings short, regular and separate from other routine meetings

Formal communication meetings are truly awful for all concerned – both you and your team will probably despise them. However, such meetings have some invaluable features. You will put them in your diary so they will tend to happen regularly. They show that you are regularly available for complaints to be made directly to you, and as a result can release pressures that are building up in the team. A common mistake is to allow the agony to drag on and on. I suggest a rigid time limit of less than an hour be adhered to.

If you have email in your team, use it to chat to them

If you have email then it is a really efficient mechanism for short, chatty updates.

Remember that communication should be a two-way process

When you make yourself available so that your team can ask you questions, you can ask them questions as well. In addition, you will probably have regular one-to-one meetings with your staff, which you can use to probe their views. If you are one of those lucky people who are naturally good listeners then this will be easy; if you are like the rest of us, keep practising those listening skills. If you organize your team to include someone who has a responsibility for staff development then that person will be a great source of feedback on the attitudes within the team, and will be able to alert you to serious concerns before they blow up into major issues.

Handling difficult staff issues

Some staff require much more management effort than others. I single out three different types of staff who require particularly careful handling. First, there are staff who are underperforming; then there are your key staff who you really do not want to lose; and lastly there are staff who take up a lot of your time but who are not really valuable to your business.

Handling underperforming staff

The first point to make is:

You must tell your staff if they are underperforming.

This may sound obvious, but you might be surprised how many managers do not face up to this task. There are, however, good ways to do this and bad ways:

When disciplining, or firing, someone, do it 'by the book'.

Much of this section describes how to help someone get over their problems, but you must always be aware of the fact that the situation could get to a stage where you need to instigate formal proceedings against one of your underperforming staff. Different countries have different laws governing unfair dismissal. Different organizations have different processes for handling underperforming staff. Find out exactly what your company processes are and follow them to the letter. If you have a good personnel department, they will probably be able to offer you support and advice. There are times to do things by the book, and this is one of them!

Identify the cause of the problem

There are two key issues to determine: first, is the staff member aware of the problem and, second, is there an underlying problem or is there a less excusable reason such as laziness or poor timekeeping? If the person is to blame then they need to be told firmly to behave. Otherwise, you need to ensure that you both understand the problem, decide how you can help, and then tell them how you expect them to address the problem.

When supplying constructive criticism you must not blame the person

The purpose of explaining a person's failings to them is to help them address the problems caused by those failings. If you blame them for their failings they are very unlikely to listen to any constructive criticism. Many of the readers of this book will themselves work in a *blame culture*. If you know that your managers will blame you for failure then you will naturally try to cover things up, and will avoid taking risks. Make sure you do not fall into the trap of creating a blame culture in your team. It is worth remembering that a blame culture happens by default – if you do not actively fight against a blame culture then that is what you will get.

Set achievable, measurable targets for improvement

It is important that underperforming staff know precisely what is expected of them. Targets must be sensibly challenging and the achievement of them easy to measure.

Do not bear a grudge

After disciplining a staff member or giving constructive criticism, both you and the person concerned may feel uncomfortable in dealing with each other. You must set the tone by dealing with them as if nothing had happened. If the person sulks then you need to decide whether it's best to ignore it, or whether they would respond to you having a quiet word with them to reinforce the fact that you are trying to help them to recognize a problem and to learn from it.

A person's failings are often the flip side of a strength

For example, someone with great personal drive may be impatient of others with less drive. In such circumstances you should acknowledge the positive attribute and suggest that the negative aspects are recognized and managed by the individual, even though they are unlikely to ever totally overcome their failings.

Never undermine a person's self-respect

Respect is key to a healthy team – both respect for self and respect for each other. Just because someone is not thriving in their current job in your team does not mean that they would not blossom if given a different job; or moved to a different team; or moved out of your organization.

Have a consistent view of how patient you will be with underperformers, and beyond that act ruthlessly

Staff need to know that they have a reasonable amount of time to address problems. They also need to know you will properly analyze the reasons for underperformance and address those causes, even if it means a move of job, or a change of manager, or some other remedy. However, your team cannot carry passengers indefinitely – they are a potential threat to the survival of the team. In addition, it is not kind to leave a person struggling – almost everyone wants to do a good job, so the person involved is probably unhappy. Once you have decided that the person has been given sufficient time to improve, you need to decide, with appropriate consultation with your superiors and/or personnel department, whether the person is redeployed or fired. If the person is to be fired:

Tell the person quickly that they are to leave and mention any positive points

Do not allow the interview to become protracted. The person will probably be in shock, so get it over with as quickly as possible. If you can give a reference, or you believe that the person has qualities that will allow them to prosper in another organization, then say so. Remember to find out from the personnel department what administrative details need to be dealt with, such as handing back passes and keys.

Make sure you use any probationary period to weed out underperformers

It is astonishing how many underperformers were spotted during a probationary period but managed to make it through on to the permanent staff. In many countries and many organizations it is vastly easier to fail a probationer than fire an underperformer.

Many managers worry how the team will react to firm management action against underperformers. Provided you allow a reasonable time for improvement, you may well be surprised that most team members would be more ruthless than you are – after all, they have to carry the passengers.

Handling your key staff

Why should you handle your key staff any differently from the rest of your team? Your innate feelings of fairness will probably lead you in the direction of 'equal treatment for all'. An additional benefit of equality of treatment is that you will defuse internal tensions caused by accusations of favouritism. However, there are differences that you should acknowledge:

- Key staff will often have superstar qualities and, as mentioned earlier, there is often a negative flip side to great qualities. It is only reasonable that you are willing to invest management time in helping with the negative aspects of genius. In my own world of research scientists there is a common saying that the line between genius and insanity is often blurred – this is a total lie . . . *line, what line?!*
- Key staff will usually know their value to you, and will often be tempted to use that power to their advantage. Anyone else trying this trick is very easy to deal with!

The key issue to decide is how far you are willing to go to keep your key staff happy. I offer the following suggestions.

Do not pretend that you are not dependent on your key staff

I have seen managers try to downplay the value of their most important people – do managers really think their top people are that stupid? It is certainly true that no one is indispensable, and that in extremis the team will survive, but do not try to minimize the value of your key staff.

Keep a dialogue going with your key staff

Most staff leave their jobs as the result of some small issue that becomes the straw that breaks the camel's back. Keeping close contact with your key staff will not only spot the 'straws', but will also allow you to keep the 'backs' from getting near to breaking point. Staff will usually drop hints about grievances, so you need to be on the lookout for problems. Sorting out such problems is much easier and cheaper if they are handled before the situation reaches crisis point. It is obviously important that you recognize who your key people are. Remember they are not just the flashy superstars; do not overlook the quieter types who are key to keeping your business alive.

A good team culture is the best protection

If your key staff value the respect of the other team members, they will not want to lose that respect by being overly demanding. A gentle 'I am worried how that will look to the rest of the team' can sometimes work wonders.

Do not yield to threats

You have to decide how far you are going to go to keep your key staff, and then be consistent in sticking to your line. Most organizations will not pay a salary that matches what a poacher will offer. In my view you cannot respond to a threat to leave by matching the poaching salary – it will cause such dissent among your other key staff that the situation will quickly get out of hand. Your best hope is to find that some other issue started the person looking outside in the first place, and that by addressing that initial grievance you can turn them around.

Do some 'succession planning'

I am not a great believer in planning for all contingencies, but particularly when a key staff member is putting pressure on you, it is worth working out how you would handle the situation if they left. Although I am recommending investing lots of effort in keeping your key staff happy, it is important to know when it is right to let them go.

When you lose a key member of the team, do it with a good grace

It is surprising how often your paths are likely to cross again. They may even want to have their old job back. There is almost no situation in which you benefit from someone leaving your team on bad terms with you.

Handling low-value/high-maintenance staff

Your key staff will often require significant investment in your time, but in most cases you will invest this time willingly because of their value to your business. There will be other staff who also require a lot of your time, but who are of only marginal value to your business. There are staff who will constantly moan about the way you and your organization treat them. There are staff who think they are much better than they really are, and who will never understand why their talents are not appreciated. There are people whose personalities cause them to fan the discontent of others. You can probably add plenty of other types of personality to this list! How do you deal with such staff?

The most obvious solution to this problem is to avoid it in the first place. Try to spot such staff during your recruitment processes and not hire them. If you spot one of these staff during a probationary period, and cannot cure their problem, then fail the probation.

No matter how hard you try, you will get problem staff who are not key to your business. The first thing to do is to work out if their problem can be solved, even partially, by making them aware of the problem. If so, then this is the place to start. There will, however, be staff whose fundamental personality traits mean they will be a constant problem. An example of this sort of person is the staff member who thinks they are much better than they really are.

What do you do about the high-maintenance, low-value staff? I recommend you calculate whether they are worth the management effort. If not, then you can either be ruthless about rationing the amount of time you spend on them, and/or you can look for every opportunity to move them out of your team. For example, you can tell someone who thinks they are better than they really are that you do not have as high an opinion of them as they have of themselves, and that maybe they need to find a different environment in which they can reach their full potential. If you find these ideas too brutal then you can carry your problem staff and hope they eventually leave. This is fine, provided that their problems only affect *you*; if they are the bad apples in your team barrel then I urge you to be brutal.

It is very important that you do not give in to this sort of person in order to keep them quiet. You must not give them higher pay rises than they deserve, and you must not give in to unreasonable demands. If you do, you deserve the discontent you will get from the rest of your team.

Staff development

Although I have serious doubts about the value of formal career development plans, I am convinced of the need to do regular appraisals of staff performance. Your organization may mandate annual appraisals, but even if it does not, you should review the performance of staff at least once a year. I tend to perform such appraisals in the run-up to salary reviews. There are a number of different aspects that can be included in such an appraisal but I think there is one issue that dominates all others:

> *Are there some aspects of a person's performance that you feel they should improve?*

If there is some way that an individual can improve their worth to the organization, they are entitled to be told about it. It sounds obvious, but time and again I see managers failing in this duty.

In a staff appraisal I try to give the person being appraised a thumbnail sketch of what I consider to be their strengths and weaknesses. I look back over their past year's performance and say what I feel they did particularly well and highlight any areas where they failed to meet my expectations. I then discuss with the person whether they feel my assessment is fair. You need to find out whether you both have the same perceptions. I also probe the individual for any aspirations they might have for the future, for example, what challenges would particularly excite them. At the end of the discussion we will decide together if any particular action needs to be taken to improve the individual's performance or their enjoyment of work.

Given that I do not believe that brilliant managers rely on formal career development processes, the next section describes the key technique that brilliant managers use.

The right job, for the right person, at the right time

Allocating staff to the right jobs should be one of a manager's highest priorities. Regrettably the commonest form of allocating staff can be summed up as:

'I have a job that needs doing; Natasha is free; she can do it.'

Or, putting it another way:

'I have a square hole; I have a round peg; pass me a hammer.'

The problem with doing it properly is that you make yourself a lot more work:

'I have a square hole; the square pegs are already in use; use one of the square pegs which fits particularly well; one of my triangular pegs could grow to fit that newly available square hole; but that triangular peg is currently in use; . . .'

Growing a staff member's capabilities is largely achieved by finding the right job to stretch them at the appropriate time. To do this you must understand what are the particular strengths of each member of your team, and choose jobs for them that utilize and grow those strengths. I am often sur-

I have a square hole; I have a round peg; pass me a hammer

prised, and dismayed, how often people are deployed on jobs that do not play to their strengths. Indeed, it often seems to be a policy to give people jobs that play to their weaknesses, in the mistaken belief that this will help them strengthen one of their weak areas.

Know it, do it, say it

Credit and blame

There is a very simple rule to follow:

The team gets all the credit, you get all the blame

If the team screws up, you can criticize your own staff, but do not allow any of your superiors to do so – they can shout at you, not your team.

An open door is not enough

It has become traditional for managers to tell their team that 'my door is always open'. I suggest that a much more powerful message to tell your team is:

> *You **must** tell me when you are unhappy or have a grievance.*

This will help create an environment in which your staff do not bottle up their unhappiness or anger.

When you make a mistake, apologize.

When was the last time your boss apologized to you? An apology, genuinely offered, will usually be accepted. Knowing that you can apologize when you make mistakes can be a great stress reducer for you. Go on, give it a try! This is a special case of the more general rule that follows.

Manners maketh managers

Can anyone tell me why so many managers seem to ignore the demands of common courtesy? What your mother taught you about saying *please* and *thank you* applies equally to the workplace as it does to your social and family lives. Remember to praise staff who have done a job well. The golden rule of management also tells you that by being courteous yourself, courtesy will become an integral part of the team culture.

Keep your promises to your staff

On the surface this sounds obvious, but the issues become clearer if it is reworded as *do not make promises you cannot keep*. Remember how busy you are and avoid the temptation to offer things that you are not sure you will have the time to deliver on. Most broken promises are not deliberate; nor are they broken because you could not deliver; they are broken because you were too busy to deliver. The best solution is not to have made the promise in the first place.

Do not trust the wrong people

I know this is not a very helpful comment to make – how do you know who to trust? There are basically two ways to find out who to trust: first, you can be a good judge of character and, second, you can see who is respected by the team. The second method only requires sufficient contact with the team and competent observational skills, and I recommend it to you. One of the most common mistakes I have seen new managers fall into is to develop a close and trusting relationship with someone the team does not respect.

Avoid giving your staff unpleasant surprises

If you have to do something that a staff member is not going to like, try to ensure it does not come 'out of the blue'. For example, make sure you have discussed with staff what the outcome of a pay review is likely to be before they receive formal notification of their pay increase. Another example is that if you are going to have to formally warn a member of the team about underperformance, make sure they know well in advance that there are concerns about their performance. Staff can easily, and justifiably, feel aggrieved if unpleasant things happen to them without any warning.

Try to avoid inconsistent behaviour

Behaviour that can be interpreted as inconsistent will greatly undermine your authority with your team. In a number of places in this book I am advocating that you take hard, and at times ruthless, action. It is important that you maintain a reputation of 'hard but fair'. The two ways to do this are: first, apply the golden rule of management and be as hard, or harder, on yourself as you are on others; second, ensure that you are consistent, and hence even-handed, in your treatment of your staff.

Never set unrealistic deadlines

I am even opposed to so-called *stretch* deadlines. Such research as there is in my field of expertise (computer software) tends to back up my own observation that tight deadlines demotivate, and unrealistic deadlines totally demotivate.

Research even shows that self-imposed tight deadlines lead to demotivation. This observation may seem to be counter-intuitive, but I suggest you try some experiments.

Choose the team's targets and incentives very carefully

Targets and incentives do motivate particular forms of behaviour, and well-chosen targets and incentives can work extremely well. However, do not be surprised if your team responds to any targets and incentives you set, to the single-minded exclusion of everything else. Some managers seem to love setting lots of targets and offering numerous incentives as a means of motivating staff; I just wish they would realize that targets and incentives are a very crude mechanism that often lead to behaviour patterns that are not in the team's interest.

I can illustrate this effect with a real example. It is not uncommon to incentivize a salesman by the volume of business they bring in. If you do this then do not expect the salesman to push very hard for the best possible price. If you want to preserve your margins, you have got to have some incentives on the price the salesman is selling for.

Never pretend you know more than you do

Some managers hate admitting they do not know something. The team will respect you much more if you freely admit your ignorance and ask to be informed. Asking stupid questions is a sign that you are not stupid.

Do not tolerate office politics within the team

Office politics, and the ambitious, small-minded people who play such games, can quickly undermine a good team spirit. I suggest you stamp hard on the first signs of politics infecting your team. A good sign of staff playing politics is when they do not behave in an obvious, straightforward way; if you cannot see what the motivation is for someone's actions, it can be worth checking what they are up to.

You have to empower people to do things differently from you, and to possibly fail

Empowerment is a much-abused word. You must think carefully beforehand whether you are delegating a task that you can afford to have done badly. You need a clear view of how you are going to check the progress being made on the delegated task and the extent to which the person doing the task is being overseen. Too often a task is delegated and then at a later date the manager panics and puts in a detailed review process. It is a sad fact that most people only learn through their own mistakes, so you have to eventually let people have the full responsibility for a task – just make sure it is a task whose failure you can recover from.

A second aspect of real empowerment is that you have to school yourself not to interfere if someone does a task very differently from the way you would have done it. If you see problems with the way they are doing a job then you may wish to alert them to the possible dangers, but if they are responsible then they must make the final choice of how to do the job.

Catch-22: you have to give trust before it has been earned

This is a corollary of the last point. Your staff will not grow until they have made the mistakes that all inexperienced staff have to make for themselves. You have to be tolerant of these mistakes, provided that people are not making the same mistake over and over again. The upshot of this is that you have to give trust to staff who have not yet earned that trust, because if you do not they will never grow to become trustworthy people.

Know when not to go to meetings

This is yet another corollary of empowerment. As the boss you will often be invited to meetings relating to tasks you have delegated others in your team to lead on. You must remember that your presence will often significantly change the nature of a meeting, and people will naturally look to you for leadership. Consequently, your presence can easily undermine the empowerment you have given to team members.

You may need to overreact

It is all too easy to underestimate how hard and fast you need to react to staff problems. It is fairly obvious that issues such as harassment, discrimination and health and safety will need strong and rapid responses. It is less obvious that problems such as underperformance, staff morale and retention can deteriorate very rapidly indeed. Provided you do not overreact to everything, thereby giving the impression of panic, overreaction seldom does harm, but underreaction can have very serious consequences.

Benign neglect: a useful technique

I have just flagged the need to be alert to the possibility that you will have to react hard and fast to certain problems. Surprisingly, the opposite technique can also be very useful. In certain circumstances, for example when people are getting overly emotional, it can be very useful to move very slowly. Managers are often *action-oriented* personalities and it can be quite hard to just leave a problem alone and let nature take its course. Unfortunately there is no magic test to distinguish those problems that need a rapid response from those that will benefit from benign neglect – it is something you can only learn through experience.

It's OK to have fun

Managing your staff is much easier if you can inject some informality and humour into your interpersonal relationships with your team. You may need to consciously make yourself relax a bit. As a member of a race of compulsive anal-retentives I know what I am talking about.

So many work environments are high-pressured these days, and so many managers are overworking and stressed out, it is

It's okay to have fun

all too easy to take all the fun out of work. Remember there is more to your working life than your pay cheque, and loosen up a bit.

Speaking of the fact there is more to life than work . . .

Drawing the line between work and home

There is no right place to draw the line between your work and your home life. If I see a tendency it is for people to allow the demands of work to cut deeper and deeper into the time you should be devoting to your family and social activities. I suggest you 'draw a line in the sand' between work and home, and try to stick to it.

It is very possible you will draw your line between work and home in a place that some in your team will find uncomfortable. Because of the golden rule of management, your team will by default take your line as the line you want everyone to adopt. I suggest you make it very clear that everyone has to draw their own line and that, within reason, you will respect their decisions and not undermine those decisions by constantly pressuring them to work anti-social hours. One of the less desirable features of a strong culture is that it can coerce people to do things they are not comfortable with; a long-hours culture is one of the commonest examples of this effect that I have seen.

Beware of sex

There is a well-recognised link between sex and power, so there is a real danger of there being a sexual undertone between yourself and team members of the opposite sex. Hence the following puritan rules:

No flirting of any sort with team members of the opposite sex.

No sexual comments or jokes of any kind.

No casual touching.

If disciplining a staff member of the opposite sex, make sure you have a witness present (e.g. from personnel).

Beware of late one-to-one meetings with staff members of the opposite sex.

And definitely no sexual relationships with team members.

Should you be foolish enough to ignore this last rule then tell your boss about the relationship immediately.

This advice is written from the viewpoint of countries where there is a serious risk of complaints of sexual harassment. Readers need to interpret my advice in the light of the prevailing conditions – what is acceptable in Italy is different from what is acceptable in the UK, which is different from the situation in the US. I would, however, point out that in all countries the situation seems to be moving in a direction where managers need to be very careful.

Harassment and discrimination: take a no-tolerance approach

Many countries now have stringent anti-harassment and anti-discrimination legislation covering issues such as gender, race and disability. In some countries employees suing for harassment or discrimination has become a growth industry. You must play any harassment or discrimination allegations, against yourself, against a member of your team, or made by a member of your team, *by the book.* Know your organization's procedures, notify your boss and the personnel department immediately, and be scrupulous in following procedures.

You need to give a strong lead, and also to protect yourself, so:

> *Almost all comments or jokes about sensitive issues such as gender and race are unacceptable.*
>
> *Disapprove immediately you hear any such comments or jokes from team members.*

Remember to check your processes, e.g. recruitment, for possible complaints of discrimination.

Summary

This chapter, more than any other, is a collection of the techniques that will help make you a brilliant manager. Most of them, I think you will instinctively know, make sense. The less obvious aspects of this chapter are:

- Managing staff involves facing difficult issues, particularly the problems of underperforming staff. The only way to handle these problems is in a tough but fair manner. Be polite; treat people with respect; but expect high standards.

- It is worth investing time in managing your key staff properly.
- Getting the allocation of the right people to the right jobs is key to developing staff.
- Make sure you give bad news personally.
- Make yourself accessible, both formally and informally, for questions from your team.
- Remember – **the team gets all the credit, you get all the blame.**

CHAPTER 2

Leadership

This is the chapter I have had most difficulty writing. What is leadership, and why is it so frightening? I think there are a number of reasons why leadership is so scary:

- As the leader you have to ensure the survival of the team.
- Often you are having to lead people who are older and more experienced than yourself.
- The idea of exercising authority and discipline is something many people are not comfortable with.

By explaining what leadership is, debunking many of the damaging myths and giving some practical techniques, I hope to be able to take some of the fear out of this subject.

What is leadership?

At its simplest a leader sets the direction and goals for their team and leads the team towards those goals. In order to achieve this a leader needs to create a *vision* of the future, and have the *respect* and *trust* of their team so that they will willingly follow the leader.

Vision is a creative thing, but an understanding of the basics of your business is the essential bedrock on which your vision must be based. Who are the team's customers? What does your team do that is valued by those customers? How do your customers and your organization measure the performance of your team?

Respect comes from getting things done. Actions speak louder than words, and achievement speaks louder than actions. People respect competence and professionalism in a leader.

Trust comes from honesty and openness, and from your actions matching your words. It also comes from your willingness to face difficult issues.

Obviously a leader has many different roles to perform. The leader is the person who makes the tough decisions. The leader is creating a community, or culture, within the team. The leader creates the organization within that community and decides who has authority within the team. The leader must care for the welfare of their staff. The leader is the interface between the team and the rest of the organization, and the figurehead of the team as far as customers are concerned. This book addresses all these different leadership roles. This chapter concentrates on how your actions affect your role as leader. It points out a range of common misconceptions about leadership, and describes common mistakes leaders make and a range of techniques that will help you become a better leader.

Leadership: the bank account concept

I expect many readers are beginning to feel a bit daunted by the thought of what they have to do to create a vision and earn the respect and trust of their staff. Can anyone live up to the standards I am describing? Of course the answer is no; even brilliant leaders have their off days. A good way to think about leadership is that when you do something right you bank some credibility with your team that you can draw on at a later date. The bad news is that your deposits (the good things you do) count for less than your withdrawals (your mistakes), so it is easy to go bankrupt; the good news is that you can make some mistakes without totally losing your credibility as the leader.

Leadership myths exposed

The first common misconception about leadership is that leaders must 'look the part'. The notion that leaders should be in the mould of the comic book hero with the square jaw, steady gaze and firm handshake is complete nonsense. The golden rule tells you that leadership is about what you do and is not about appearances.

Leaders with charismatic personalities have an advantage in the early days of taking over a team, but if you are such a person you need to be aware of a range of dangers that charismatic leaders are prone to:

- Charismatic leaders tend to create personality cults. Teams can become overdependent on the leader and often there is very poor planning for when the leader leaves.
- Charismatic leaders are often poor at delegating.
- Charismatic leaders are often poor listeners; they spend all their time talking.
- Charismatic leaders often have poor self-awareness and hence are not aware of their limitations.
- Charismatic leaders often depend on their personalities to get them out of trouble, so they are not careful enough about avoiding getting into trouble.
- Charismatic leaders are often workaholics and get very tired and make too many mistakes.

A second common myth is that leaders need to rely on the authority given to them by the organization. Sure, as the boss you can order people to do things, but as a leader you should seldom have to issue a direct order. If you are doing your job properly, your team should want to follow you.

A common failing of authoritarian leaders is that they tend to behave in ways that ensure that nothing is allowed to undermine their authority. Typical examples might be:

- not seeking advice from the team;
- not changing their mind even when they are wrong;
- delegating very little to avoid diluting their power, and constantly undermining anyone with delegated authority;
- recruiting staff of sufficiently low quality that they will never be a threat;
- using fear, uncertainty and doubt, and divide-and-conquer as management techniques to avoid threats to their authority.

I leave the completion of this list as an exercise for the reader.

I doubt if any authoritarian leaders would ever want to read this book, but it is worth producing this parody because most of us have a small part of our personalities that worries about someone challenging our authority. This means that we may hear a quiet, insidious voice encouraging us not to recruit the outstanding candidate, or not to reverse a poor decision.

It is worth examining the point about reversing bad decisions in a little bit more detail. This is an example of a management *paradox* – a word from an obscure dialect of English called *management-speak*. A paradox is used to describe the not uncommon situation when two factors are in direct conflict.

In this situation, it is desirable to change a bad decision, but consistency and stability of direction are desirable for maintaining staff morale. The resolution of this paradox is to ensure that the basic tenets of the business strategy remain reasonably constant, but tactics can change much more frequently.

Personality cults revisited

In the last section I alerted charismatic leaders to the dangers of creating a personality cult. This effect is not limited to just charismatic personalities. One side effect of the golden rule of management is that your personality traits will become part of your team's culture. If you are highly competitive, your team will most likely be very competitive. If you are a generous person then your team will probably be generous. If you are a caring person then your team will have a caring culture. If you act the bully . . . you have probably got the message. This is quite an alarming observation because it means your personality defects are likely to become team defects. I can offer two techniques for avoiding such problems.

Faking it

Much of our behaviour is learned rather than natural. True, we did most of our learning when young, but there is no reason at all why you cannot learn new behaviour patterns. This is easiest for detailed behaviour patterns. For example, if you are naturally careful with your money, it is fairly easy to make yourself put your hand in your pocket and make sure you buy more than your fair share of drinks at social gatherings. Many of the suggestions I make in this book can be easily implemented by making a conscious effort – for example, I will recommend that you be courteous to your support staff, and there is no reason at all why you cannot make the effort to be polite.

There are two important questions: first, won't your staff spot that you are faking it and, second, is it possible to change fundamental characteristics of your personality? Taking these in order:

1 Of course your team will spot you are acting, but they are likely to admire you for it. They will see it as an effort on your part to behave well. Perhaps more scary is that you will probably start off being a bad actor and then, with practice, you will become a good actor and, finally, you may find you are no longer acting!

2 The technique works best on detailed aspects of your behaviour. It is much harder to adapt your behaviour when a fundamental aspect of your personality is involved. For example, a hypercompetitive personality is going to find it hard not to be competitive, but it is certainly possible to temper such traits. Being aware of your less desirable personality traits is half the way to solving the problem.

Delegate areas of weakness

Say you find your abilities or personality wanting in an important area. For example, you may find it hard to create a credible vision of the future, or your interpersonal skills mean that you find it hard to deal with staff problems. As the leader it is your job to ensure that all the bases are covered, not necessarily that you do everything yourself. In such cases it is best that you either seek support from members of your team who have the necessary talents, or formally delegate those roles to them. This is a specific example of the importance that good leaders give to organizing their teams.

Organizing your team

The best leaders invest a lot of effort in organizing their team to work efficiently. In the 'Suggested reading' section at the end of this chapter there is a book called *Built to Last* that describes this issue in great detail. A later chapter is devoted to this subject, but I would like to highlight a few key issues now.

Be careful to trust the right people

The simplest technique to use is to observe who is well respected by the team. They should be the first people you consider trusting.

Delegate properly

Delegation is one of the hardest issues a leader faces. You must consider up front the constraints that you want to impose on the use of delegated authority. Ideally you want to let people get on with their delegated roles with the minimum of interference from you. However, the ultimate responsibility for all mistakes rests with you, not with your team members – you must insist that your bosses shout at you and never shout directly at your staff. Your superiors must accept that it is your responsibility, and your responsibility alone, to ensure that problems get sorted.

You will want to maintain an appropriate level of visibility so that major problems can be caught in time to take remedial action; but you do not want to introduce a stifling bureaucracy; and your staff have to learn by their mistakes; but you must provide an appropriate level of advice and support to inexperienced staff; and you must allow people to do tasks differently from how you would have done them . . . I told you it was hard!

Deploying your key people

Within any team there tend to be relatively few staff who are a 'safe pair of hands'. There also tend to be relatively few staff who you can throw a problem at and be sure they will sort it out. Likewise, there tend to be relatively few staff who can be totally trusted to interact with the customer and make a good impression. Making sure that you have the right staff in the right jobs is one of the keys to creating an efficient organization.

Lightweight management processes

When mistakes happen it is all too easy to get into a mindset of creating a new quality process to avoid that mistake happening again. There is a natural tendency for such bureaucracy to grow and grow. It takes a positive effort to set up a system where people can get on with their jobs with the minimum of administrative overhead while retaining sufficient visibility that mistakes are usually spotted before they become a serious problem. Good *leadership* can create an organization that has a minimum of *management* overhead.

The youthful leader's problems

Most youthful managers face the daunting prospect of having authority over staff who are much older and more experienced than themselves. The first thing to be aware of is that you are probably more worried than they are. You are probably not the first young manager they have had to train, and most experienced staff will not try to embarrass or undermine you – provided you follow a few simple rules.

Use the experience within your team

Experienced staff will expect to be consulted. If you do not seek their views they will think that you are either arrogant or insecure. Ultimately you must make the decisions yourself, but you should make well-informed decisions.

You should also consider organizing your team to make best use of the experience available to you.

Try to avoid snap decisions soon after taking over

When taking over a team try to give yourself time to find out about the team, its business and some of its history before trying to change things.

Be very careful when criticizing experienced staff

If you need to discuss a shortcoming in an experienced team member's performance make it clear that you are being very careful to get your facts right. This is potentially the most embarrassing situation of all. If you are careful to treat the staff member with respect and show that you are trying to find out what went wrong so that they can learn the lessons from the experience, they will probably help you by criticizing themselves first.

When to move on, how to move on

Different circumstances call for different leadership styles. For example, turning round a failing team requires a very different approach from growing a successful team, which requires a different approach from running a team that is neither growing nor contracting . . . and so on. You need to watch for a team moving from one state to another, because at the very least you will have to adapt your leadership style, and it may be that you need to move aside and let a new leader take over.

The very best leaders design an organization that is not overly dependent on their own personal skills and will think about succession planning to ensure a smooth transition to new leadership at the appropriate time.

Know it, do it, say it

This whole book is about being a good leader and a good manager. This section highlights some techniques that you might overlook for enhancing your image as a leader, and some mistakes that will damage your reputation.

Don't be afraid to roll your sleeves up and help

Many managers used to do some of their team members' roles before they became a manager. Even if your professional expertise is not in the areas of the team's business, you undoubtedly have some relevant skills to contribute – be they presentational, organizational or business related. Working alongside your team delivering value to your customers will show you a view of your team you cannot get from just being the boss, and can greatly increase the respect the team have for you.

Don't think you are too important to do menial jobs

A willingness to do menial jobs, such as washing up your own coffee cup, will strengthen, not undermine, your authority.

The team get all the credit, you get all the blame

It may not be fair, but that's the rule of the game. Repeating the point, you must not allow your superiors to shout directly at your staff; you must insist they deal with you, and you will sort it out. If there are any beatings to be handed out, you must do it personally. Your staff have a right to expect your support in dealings with the rest of the organization.

Self-serving behaviour destroys trust

The previous point about passing credit on to the team is a specific case of this more general point. If your team detect that furthering your career is one of your top priorities, they will never trust you. If you are very ambitious you need to decide if your long-term interests are best served by being a good leader, and if you decide they are you will need to avoid crude, short-term tactics for promoting yourself.

Admit your mistakes and apologise when necessary

Too many managers worry about losing face and try to cover up their mistakes; your reputation can only be enhanced by putting your hands up and saying sorry. If you are making so many mistakes that this is not a credible strategy then it is time to try a different job you are better suited to.

Be honest and talk straight

It is all too easy to get sucked into 'being economical with the truth'. If you are to keep people's respect it is far better, and less complicated, to stick to the truth. It is also easy to start avoiding the question and to start acting like a politician – and how many politicians do you trust? Possibly the only time the staff will tolerate dissembling is when you are obliged to defend the corporate line; how far you go in backing the corporate line is very dependent on your personality.

Do not try to be liked

Do not confuse being respected with being liked. It is essential that a leader be respected, and irrelevant if you are liked. Courting popularity is an excellent recipe for not being respected. Moving on to a related problem . . .

Do not try to be 'one of the gang'

Regrettably the trite comment about the loneliness of leadership has some truth behind it. As a leader you can never fully be one of the team and at social gatherings the rest of the team will quite correctly never completely forget you are the leader. This means that there are some social gatherings that you must attend, such as the Christmas party, but it is usually best to decline invitations to ad hoc social gatherings – they really do not want the boss there. Do not take it personally if you are not invited.

Avoid all forms of bullying behaviour

I hope I do not have to convince the reader that overt bullying is a bad trait. Less obvious are the subtle forms of bullying:

- talking over people;
- losing your temper frequently;
- pressuring people to work anti-social hours;
- having unreasonable expectations, for example in expecting people to completely reorganize their schedules in response to a serious problem;
- showing a lack of respect;
- being impolite.

Be visible

A leader who is not highly visible cannot be a good leader. You must avoid spending too much time away from the team – this will probably mean declining many requests for your presence at meetings that take you out of the office. When in the office make sure you spend enough time talking to staff face to face. It is a good idea to make yourself available for ad hoc questions, for example by occasionally having coffee or lunch with the team.

Communicate your vision of the future

It is not good enough for you to have a clear vision of the future – your team must buy into it. Just writing it down and circulating it is not good enough. You have to involve the team in its creation and make sure that your actions show that the vision is something that affects your decisions.

Never imply a job you do not do, or cannot do, is easy

If you do not respect your staff they will not respect you. If you are sitting there thinking that of course you respect your staff, just check that you have not said anything like the following:

'Surely all you need to do is . . .'

'This shouldn't take you long . . .'

'I've got an easy job I would like you to do for me . . .'

'Surely it won't take that long . . .'

'Don't bother me with details . . .'

'It's only a small change . . .'

'I think this will solve your problem . . .'

'I've seen this wonderful new . . .'

'We can get the new recruit to do that . . .'

'I can do that on my PC at home . . .'

'Stop raising difficulties . . . I want solutions, not problems'

Beware the easy compromise

One of your jobs as leader is to make the hard decisions. It is also your role to actively seek out problems by asking challenging questions. Often the seemingly reasonable approach of trying to find the middle ground, and making a measured response, will just delay the inevitable disaster. You need to be alert to the circumstances when you need to get off the fence and make a stand. In my experience it is more common to make a mistake by underreacting than by overreacting. It is also my experience that staff are often very supportive of clear, decisive action in the appropriate circumstance.

Do not micro-manage

You must give your staff space to grow their abilities. If you do not trust them, they will never trust you.

Consistency and predictability breed trust

I know this is an obvious comment, but it is so important that I felt it should be included. Often the best way to achieve predictability is to have a strong set of basic principles and then use those principles to guide your actions. It is an approach that can lead to a strong team culture, and is discussed further in the next chapter.

Summary

Leadership is knowing where you want the team to go, and having enough credibility with the team that they will follow you in that direction.

There is a strong moral dimension to leadership. If you do right by your team, they will trust you. Your team will accept that you have flaws but you must get enough things right in order to keep their trust and respect. This chapter describes many things you should do, and many things you should not do, if you want to be trusted and respected. I believe that one of the distinguishing features of human beings is that they can choose to modify their behaviour. I also suspect that if you are reading this book you are the sort of person who wants to improve your performance, so you may be willing to try out some new approaches.

Your good qualities will permeate the team. Unfortunately your weaknesses can easily infect the team. You can try to modify your behaviour to mask your weaknesses but you have an additional weapon at your disposal – you can organize the team so that other team members take on the roles that you are less able to perform well. In order to do this you must be willing to do a bit of self-analysis and have the courage to admit to yourself where you have flaws and weaknesses.

Suggested reading

Collins, James C. and Jerry I. Porras (2004) *Built to Last: Successful Habits of Visionary Companies*: New York, Harperbusiness.

A very well-researched book that examines what distinguishes the very best companies from other good companies. Although the subject matter is about large organizations many of the lessons apply to small teams as well.

CHAPTER 3

Culture

One of the signs that you are getting it right as a manager is when your team behaves as you want without being supervised or explicitly instructed to do so. A strongly defined culture within the team is an excellent way of achieving this desirable state. If team members instinctively know 'this is the way we do things' and 'we don't do things like that' then team members will tend to act in ways you approve of, and avoid doing things you would disapprove of. More than that, there will be peer pressure within the team for everyone to behave in ways that are compatible with the team culture. Another desirable consequence of the team culture reinforcing your own principles is that team members will be able to easily predict how you would react to a particular set of circumstances. Hearing someone say 'I knew you would do that' is not an indication that you are unimaginative and dull, but should be taken as a compliment of the highest order.

So how do you achieve a good, strong culture? Reiterating the golden rule of management in a slightly different form:

> *Consistent behaviour by the leader sets the tone for the culture.*

I have included the word *consistent* to stress that inconsistent behaviour will very rapidly produce a dysfunctional culture. Almost as bad will be if your words and your actions are inconsistent – in such cases your actions will set the culture, but your personal standing will be severely undermined.

Understand the existing culture

The chances are that you took over the running of an existing team. You need to understand what culture you have inherited and, in particular, what aspects of the culture are highly valued by your staff. Changing any aspect of the existing culture will need skilful and honest handling. Generally speaking, a wise new manager takes their time to understand a new team and avoids rapid changes of direction. A second influence on your team's culture will be if your organization has strong cultural traits. For example, if you work for an aggressive and combative organization, you will have difficulty if you try to create a culture that runs directly counter to this organizational bias.

I will split the remainder of the chapter into two parts. The first will be a discussion of the different sorts of culture that you may want to create. The second part will discuss what techniques you can deploy to change the culture in the directions that you want – or, alternatively, that will change the culture in ways you may not want if you do not plan your behaviour appropriately.

What sort of culture do you want?

As this book is aimed at the managers of the value creation within an organization, or those who provide a service to others who create value, many of your team will deal with customers within or outside the organization. If this is the case I strongly suggest you have strong cultural values about customer service. In the section on how to create a culture I will return to customer service as an example.

Many strong cultures have extreme aspects to them. I want to use this as an example of a common fallacy. A culture is a social system, and any soft science that grows up around such complex systems – be it management science, psychology or

Many strong cultures have extreme aspects to them

economics – is very prone to incorrect suppositions of cause and effect. The fact that strong cultures are usually extreme does not imply that by making a culture extreme you will necessarily make it strong. Other examples might be (from economics) strong economies have stable exchange rates, but forcing an exchange rate to be stable will not necessarily produce a strong economy; or (from management theory) good companies nearly always have good quality systems, but implementing a good quality system will not necessarily significantly improve your company. On the subject of extremism in cultures, all I would say is don't be afraid of making the culture extreme in pursuit of a principle you feel very strongly about. However, a word of warning: I know of very few cultures that have numerous, different extreme aspects. You will have to be highly selective about those aspects of the culture you choose to highlight in an extreme fashion.

I am suggesting that you should align the culture with your leadership principles. You will also want to consider aligning the culture to reinforce other key aspects of your management approach. In managing aspects of your business, for example customer service or the financial bottom line, you will probably have to adopt a technique described in *management-speak* as *loose/tight.* All this means is that you choose a few key factors to control tightly and will leave all the other factors under much looser control. As an example, consider the financial controls within your organization – I will bet that you can instantly identify the tight financial controls, be it capital expenditure or cash flow or staff utlization or margins or volume. You should consider which tight controls you exercise within your team are naturally suited to cultural reinforcement.

Few teams today are insulated from the need to constantly explore changes to their current operations. To encourage this you will have to develop a culture that *genuinely* tolerates honourable failure. This fact is constantly stressed by management gurus and most organizations pay lip service to this idea . . . but their actions usually betray the shallowness of their understanding of the concept of tolerating failure. Within the more narrow confines of your team you must ensure that those who fail honourably are not penalized and, if appropriate, are rewarded on pay, promotion or other tangible aspects of their careers.

Many strong cultures think of themselves as an elite. This can be a valuable attitude as it means that the culture sets itself very high standards, which will naturally tend to lead to high-quality outputs from your team. There is, however, a less positive side. Elites tend to be very insular and often regard those outside their culture as 'useless' or 'stupid'. The view of an elite from the outside often calls them 'arrogant' and 'overbearing'. By ensuring that your personal behaviour is always tolerant and respectful of people outside the culture, and by going out of your way to show you disapprove of intolerance to outsiders, you can go a long way to counteracting this natural tendency.

How to create and change a culture

How you use your own time

An implication of the golden rule is that what you spend your time doing will send a very strong message to the team about your priorities. As an example I will describe a common mistake I see time and again. Managers often involve themselves in the pursuit of new business opportunities. There is nothing wrong in this, but if it gets to the stage that you spend little or no time taking an interest in your team's existing core business and its customers then you can expect those working to generate the bulk of your income to feel thoroughly unappreciated.

Management processes

One of the most important tools you have at your disposal is the detailed design of the processes within your team. Changing processes can have a major impact on the culture. I will use a business-related example concerning the team's attitude to customer service. Consider the impact that allowing staff who interact directly with customers to have delegated authority to resolve some customer complaints 'on the spot' without reference to you or anyone else in authority. Do you trust your staff with such authority? Just how much authority are you willing to delegate? Do you think you need additional processes to manage the risk that the delegated authority will be mistakenly applied? Are your staff sufficiently aware of the big picture to exercise such authority properly? Are they sufficiently well trained to exercise such authority safely? All these issues will lead to the team members being aware of the level to which they personally are responsible for customer satisfaction, and this will quickly become ingrained as part of the cultural approach to customer service. Although this is a somewhat simplistic example it hopefully illustrates the key role that processes can play in defining the team culture.

Pay and promotion

Your implementation of staff pay and promotions will seriously impact on the culture of your team. You are bound to be constrained by organizational processes, but you must remember the fundamental rule of staff dissatisfaction:

> *Your staff will be most affected by comparison with other team members, secondly by others in the organization, and lastly by comparison with others outside the organization.*

You must ensure you treat your staff in an appropriately open and fair way when it comes to pay, promotions and bonuses. Just one bad promotion decision can have a serious impact on your credibility and a major impact on staff morale – make sure you get it right! Time invested in getting it right is time well spent. Resist the temptation to use promotions and bonuses to reward those working on your current favourite projects, everyone must be treated equally. One useful way of avoiding promoting the wrong people is to bounce your ideas for future promotions off a few of the experienced members of your team.

Recruitment

Another area I would encourage you to invest your own time in is recruitment. The sorts of staff you are trying to recruit sends a very strong message to the team. Your personal involvement will also show that you take a personal interest in the future of the team. It is also the key to the level of diversity you want the culture to tolerate. A common failing of the strong leader is to recruit clones of themselves, which reinforces the fact that the culture will tend to absorb the leader's failings anyway. As an example, consider your current staff and think which of them are best suited to starting with a project, those that are good at working on a mature project, and those that are good at finishing things off. Finishers are a rare breed and tend to be unflashy personalities. It is your job to ensure that you get an appropriately broad mix of staff into the team. A second word of warning is to ensure that you do not allow any feelings of insecurity to discourage the recruitment of outstanding staff – you must not view such staff as a threat. Just remember that good people recruit better people, while poor people recruit worse people.

Recruitment is an interesting example of how cultures can become self-perpetuating. A strongly defined culture will be attractive to like-minded recruits and will tend to repel those who would not fit in. If someone is recruited who does not fit in then a strong culture tends to expel them – not physically, but someone who does not fit in will tend not to thrive and not be really happy in the team, and will often leave of their own accord.

When designing your recruitment process the following points are worthy of consideration:

- Think carefully about the qualities and skills you are looking for and ensure that your recruitment process tests candidates for those qualities and skills.
- A full day is about the correct length of time for the initial selection process, although you may ask those that have done well, but you are not sure about, to come back for another visit.

- Hold the selection day in your normal working environment and expose the candidates to the team culture.
- Use the formal interview to test for the person's qualities (personality, motivations, judgement and ethics), not their professional expertise. An excellent technique is to ask the candidates to illustrate their answers from their own past experiences – 'Can you give me an example of how you handled a difficult person who was in authority over you?'
- Use an informal interview to probe their professional expertise and experience.
- Ask candidates to bring examples of previous work. How many times have I seen programmers being hired by organizations that have not seen one line of program written by the person?
- Ask the person to prepare a 10-minute presentation on some experience, within a work context, they found interesting. Have a small group from your team spend 10 or 15 minutes asking them questions on their presentation.
- Have a short (about 30 minutes) practical test. I have used a short case study that asked the candidate to analyze a fairly general work-related problem.
- Make sure the recruit has a one-to-one with a fairly new team member where the recruit can quiz them.

Try to handle the process as informally as possible. You want to find out about the recruit, and for the recruit to decide if they like your team. There is no reason it cannot be an enjoyable experience for the recruit – if it is fun they are much more likely to accept a job offer.

Staff retention

Retaining the staff you recruit, especially the best staff, is obviously as important as recruiting staff in the first place. Many managers underestimate the financial cost of high staff turnover. A strong culture can have a dramatic, positive effect on staff retention. Industrial psychologists have long recognized that workers are motivated by an environment that gives their working life meaning. We are also motivated by the need to feel a sense of belonging. This may all sound a bit spiritual but these are powerful forces that can generate great staff loyalty. Anyone who has earned a position of respect within a strong culture will think long and hard before giving that up to move to a new job where they will have to rebuild such a position from scratch.

Physical surroundings

The effect of physical surroundings is often underrated by managers. Although you will often be severely constrained by your organization's policies on accommodation, it is likely you can find significant 'wiggle room' to adapt the surroundings to better suit the culture you want. Maybe it is a reorganization of an open-plan office area, or maybe an informal meeting area for coffee times, or the allocation of rooms for impromptu meetings. One reason that office accommodation raises such high passions is that workers understand how important it is to their efficiency and happiness – it is a pity that more managers and organizations do not understand this as passionately.

Staying on the subject of accommodation, your personal accommodation sends a very strong message to the team. If they work in open plan and you have a nice secluded office, what do you think they will read into this? Sure, you may need to have more confidential conversations and telephone calls, but sharing the open-plan accommodation and having a small meeting room dedicated to your use sends a much more positive message. There is a (possibly apocryphal) story about a new chief executive at Hewlett-Packard arriving at his new office, and his first action was unscrewing the door and leaving it propped up against the wall. The number of times I have heard this story told is testament to the significance that physical surroundings have on a culture. The story is also a good example of how what management gurus refer to as *myths and legends* are a powerful way in which cultures become self-sustaining. As new members of the culture hear such anecdotes they receive a powerful message about the underlying principles of the culture.

Social events

A rich source of myths and legends, usually of the embarrassing kind, is team social events. The social dimension is one that must be adapted to the individual circumstances of any particular team. The only suggestion I have to offer is that if you receive a bonus based on the performance of the team, you invest part of that bonus in sponsoring some team social events.

A plea for intolerance

I will conclude this section with an unusual plea for intolerance. I suggest you are extremely intolerant of anyone who breaks the fundamental *principles* of the culture. For example, if integrity is a cornerstone of the culture then those who play fast and loose with integrity should be nailed to the wall as an example to others.

I also suggest that you avoid the temptation to turn a blind eye to minor transgressions, such as bending the rules on expenses, minor health and safety infractions and bad-taste jokes. One of the reasons that a manager cannot be 'one of the gang' is that the leader of the culture should set high standards, both in their own behaviour and by reacting each and every time they find team members bending the rules.

Summary

The principle that underlies the culture of your team is:

Consistent behaviour by the leader sets the tone for the culture

Your actions will tell the team what you approve of and what you disapprove of.

You need to be aware of the impact that the subtle signals you send will have on your team's culture. Issues such as your office accommodation, how you prioritize your time and how you react to bad news will have a significant effect on the culture of your team.

Suggested reading

DeMarco, Tom and Timothy Lister (1999), *Peopleware: Productive Projects and Teams*, 2nd edn: New York, Dorset House.

A provocative study of productivity in the software industry. It has the best, and most amusing, discussion of the effects of office accommodation on productivity that I have read.

Peters, Thomas and Robert H. Waterman (1998), *In Search of Excellence: Lessons from America's Best-Run Companies*: London, Warner Books.

Similar in scope to *Built to Last*. First published in 1982, this is a famous management book. The examples are now very dated, but the underlying analysis of company cultures is still relevant.

CHAPTER 4

Managing different types of people

Shouldn't a manager treat everyone the same? Your innate sense of decency and fairness will push you in this direction but over time I have come to realize that a brilliant manager needs to understand the particular characteristics and hang-ups of different professions.

In this chapter I will be looking at a number of different professions and analyzing what makes people who do these jobs tick. I will describe a number of techniques for having a good managerial relationship with these different professions, from very specific professions such as lawyers and software engineers, to more generic types such as support staff, sales people and creative people.

Before getting down to the details of the different types of people you have to manage and interact with, here are some fundamental principles that apply across the board.

When dealing with other professions, you need to respect their professionalism. There is absolutely no point in consulting a lawyer and then constantly arguing with them or ignoring their advice. On the other hand, professionals can often forget that their principal role is to *support* the manager in making a decision. In many cases it will be you who has to make the decision on business grounds, and it is for your experts to advise you of different possibilities and relevant implications. For example, if a creative person proposes a new product idea then you will probably have to take the lead in exploring how their idea could be adapted to bring it to market; you will pose market scenarios, but the creative person will be the one who knows best how to adapt their idea to those scenarios.

Interacting with people who are experts in different areas from yourself is a bit of an art. Here are the key points to remember.

Never show disrespect for an expert's professionalism

Many experts can try the patience of a saint! No matter how annoyed you get, you must never make the mistake of allowing your annoyance to be expressed in a disrespectful manner. For many experts, the worst of all insults is to accuse them of being unprofessional.

Do not allow yourself to be blinded by jargon

The best professionals can make themselves understood to laymen. There is a very common tendency for experts to hide behind a veneer of 'professional mystique'. Do not allow your experts to intimidate you. It is not only acceptable, it is essential that you require that experts explain their points to you in language that you can understand. If this means asking question after question after question – so be it. They will eventually get the message that you insist on understanding the issues that are relevant to the decisions you have to take.

Explain your problems to your experts

I have found that it is nearly always very productive for you to explain your problem area to your experts. It is obviously much easier for them to help you if they understand the nature of the problems you face. Experts are usually fascinated to find out how your business works. I would, however, remind you that you should not use jargon on them!

Beware of advocacy

Experts have a nasty habit of holding strong, and not entirely rational, views on some areas of their expertise. If you detect the gleam of religious fervour in your adviser's eyes then you need to be on your guard. This is one of those times when you may need to seek a second opinion.

Beware the trendy solution

Another nasty habit of various professions is to follow the latest fad. You only have to look at your own area of management to see how many managers slavishly adopt the latest quack nostrum peddled by some management guru. If you suspect this effect, ask how well established the technique is, and ask for examples of the successful use of the solution proposed.

Be suspicious when told something is impossible

Experts will seldom tell you an outright lie. However, when they say, correctly, that something is impossible, they may well know that if you changed the question slightly then you could achieve what you wanted. This is why it is so important to explore the underlying issues and not to let your experts get you bogged down in irrelevant detail. A good question to ask is, 'Is there anything I can do that will give me 80 per cent of what I want?'

Beware of self-serving advice

I have done some management consultancy in my career, so I know how difficult it is to resist the temptation to recommend that an issue needs 'further study'. It is natural for experts to want you to become dependent on their advice. Given human nature, you must take the lead in ensuring that you get the advice that is the best for you, not the best for your advisers.

Beware of advisers withholding relevant information from you

Some experts seem to work on the basis that knowledge is power, and will attempt to ration the information they give you.

It is clear from the above how careful you have to be when dealing with expert advisers; so what can you do to get the best from them? There is one key technique that the brilliant manager should always fall back on – *keep asking questions until you fully understand the issues.* Use your advisers to inform you of the relevant issues. Certainly they can offer advice on your decision, but make it clear that you make the decisions – not them.

Enough of generalities, let's get down to some detail. There is a danger in the sections that follow that you will feel that I am guilty of perpetuating offensive stereotypes about different professions. I will try to avoid being offensive, but it is my view that many professions do indeed exhibit stereotypical characteristics. I am not saying that every member of every profession displays the qualities I describe, but I think that managers can benefit from being aware of how and why different professions tend to act, and react, in particular ways. I would also point out in my defence that in my career I have at various times been a creative type, an IT person, a salesman and also a consultant – so if I am insulting such people I am also insulting myself.

Lawyers

I will start with a confession – I have greatly enjoyed my interactions with my legal experts and contracts staff and I find the law a fascinating subject. So let me start by giving their side of the story.

First off, why do people always leave it too late to consult their lawyers? If only people asked for advice in good time then life would be so much easier. Second, no one remembers the pressure the lawyer was put under to get a contract out quickly when, years later, the agreement is tested in court and found to be poorly drafted. Third, people do not understand the importance of legal issues and tend to treat lawyers as an irritating nuisance who stop them getting on with their business, rather than experts who are trying to stop the careless manager from unnecessarily risking their business. I will spare you clauses IV to XXXII of the 'lament of the lawyer', but hopefully you recognize that there is at least some truth in the three gripes I have listed. So, why is there often such a frosty relationship between the manager/businessman and the lawyer? The principal reason is that the fundamental personality traits of managers and lawyers tend to be diametrically opposed:

Managers tend to be risk-takers, while lawyers are trained to be risk-averse

I believe that managers and lawyers should openly acknowledge this fundamental divide and both sides should try to appreciate the views of the other side. The middle ground is *risk management* – your lawyer must ensure that you understand the full implications of all the risks you choose to accept.

An additional personality issue that managers need to be aware of is that *legal training reinforces adversarial personalities.* Lawyers are trained to win arguments, and so you need to be aware that most good lawyers enjoy a good fight – not to mention the fact that a good fight is usually highly profitable for lawyers.

I will finish this section with what you need to know, do and say to interact successfully with lawyers.

Lawyers seldom give short answers to questions

I have noticed that when lawyers answer a question they will frequently give a very full context to their answer, sometimes going all the way back to first principles. It is my experience that it is hopeless to resist and it is much better to listen patiently – you may even learn something new.

Don't involve lawyers directly in the early stages of business negotiations

The purpose of a legal agreement is to accurately record a deal that has been negotiated by business people. Lawyers do not have the right motivations, or the right temperaments, for business negotiations.

Regard contracts as prenuptials

One of the main services that lawyers provide is to help agree the divorce terms while both parties are still friends.

Don't let lawyers stop you handling a crisis properly

Of all the times I have found lawyers to be unhelpful, the most extreme is when there is a crisis. Lawyers, by their nature and training, like to fully research a topic before offering advice; so they react badly to having to give the snap advice needed in a crisis. A second major problem is that a crisis can often be best resolved, from a public relations perspective, by an honest admission of responsibility. Lawyers hate their clients admitting liability and, consequently, a strong business lead may be necessary to put the lawyers 'back in their box'. Once the lawyers realize that you really do intend to apologize, they will be of great use in drafting a form of words that delivers a positive PR result while minimizing financial liability.

IT staff

Unlike lawyers, the problems of dealing with IT staff are more to do with the nature of their profession than their particular personality traits. Although IT professionals use the phrase *software engineering*, it is important for the manager to understand that it is not an engineering discipline in the same way that civil engineering is. To exhaustively test anything but the simplest of computer programs takes far too much time to be practical. To use mathematics to prove the correctness of anything but the simplest of programs is beyond current technology. The effects of this mathematical 'problem' are well known:

- even the best software programs contain lots of bugs;
- software projects are prone to disastrous cost and time overruns.

There are a number of issues that managers need to be aware of when dealing with IT staff and IT projects, some of which are detailed below.

Software estimating

The first thing to say is that most IT staff are incurable optimists when it comes to estimating how much time and money a piece of software will take to complete. Given the mathematical complexity underlying software, it is not surprising that there are no reliable techniques for software estimating. As a manager you need to know the truth – the only technique that works at all well is by analogy with a past project. Comparing a project with the nearest similar project in size, complexity and functionality can give you a rough idea of time and cost. Even this technique can easily be undermined by the differences between the new project and the project being used for comparison purposes – for example, different staff abilities, or some subtle difference in functionality that proves very hard to implement. If you cannot find a good analogy then your project faces a major risk of time and cost overruns, and even with a good analogy the risks are never small. In summary:

> *Be afraid, be very afraid.*

A few additional, unhelpful hints:

- Any product vendor selling you any technique or tool that makes software development totally predictable is a liar (but the product may be worth buying anyway).
- Quality systems do not solve this problem (but they may be worth using anyway).
- Project management processes cannot solve this problem (but they may highlight the severity of the problem earlier).

Now for a helpful comment:

> *A third of the way through a software project, the staff on the project will have a very good idea how long the entire project will take – but will still be too optimistic.*

This begs the question – how much contingency should the manager add at this stage to get an accurate estimate? The best I can do is offer an observation that I have made, which is that when a software engineer says that the project is 80 per cent complete it is at most only half done. In practice I tend to add about 30 per cent to the estimates I get from staff when they are a third of the way through a project.

Although it is seldom easy, you must plan to review the deadlines and cost estimates about a third of the way through the project. IT staff become demoralized when they know they are working to impossible deadlines.

Software projects usually fail for a few well-known reasons

This following list is very relevant because you as the manager have the responsibility for most of them:

- The requirement for the software was much too ambitious. It is your duty to ensure that the team sticks to the KISS principle – Keep It Simple, Stupid! IT staff tend to love their technology and will seldom question the need for more and more computerization. This leads to the next problem.
- The requirement for the software becomes divorced from the needs of its ultimate users.
- Weak management! Managers not intervening or making decisions because they do not feel qualified to make judgements about a software project – I will be discussing this in more detail later in the section.
- Continuing acceptance of unrealistic deadlines and unwillingness to brief senior management on the underlying problems.
- Overreliance on consultants.
- Reinventing the wheel, rather than using off-the-shelf packages (and occasionally vice versa).
- Poor handling of the risks posed by suppliers and subcontractors.
- Acceptance of a big-bang introduction of the new software – always run a new system in parallel with any system being replaced. Ensure that there is a fallback mode of operation for when the software falls in a heap – because it will!

Having started this section by saying that software engineering is very different from other engineering disciplines, I look back at this list and see that most of it applies equally to any technical job.

It's the third version of software that works

Most good software engineers know that they need to rip up their software at least twice in the process of developing any substantial piece of code. Usually, they have to hide the fact that they have thrown away most of the software from their managers. Hopefully by explaining this truth to you, you can actively plan for the inevitable rewrites, and gain the respect of your IT staff in the process. Also, if you find that your IT staff do not feel that the software would benefit from a rewrite, you need to start worrying about the quality of your IT staff.

Security: a no-win for IT staff

Every profession seems to have its no-win situations, and it is worth understanding them because experts can, understandably, get emotional when you blunder into one. For IT staff, security is one of their major no-win issues. Businesses are very loath to invest in proper IT security, but are quick to shoot the IT experts when security is breached. Please listen carefully when your IT staff discuss security issues.

Managers' roles in IT projects

Although you may know little or nothing about how to write software, your expertise, judgement and leadership is vital in a number of areas, as follows:

Ensure that the functional specification of the software is appropriate to the needs of your business

It is a well-known fact in the IT industry that many of the problems in software projects stem from mistakes made in the requirements that the software has to meet. I have already mentioned the importance of KISS; you must constantly battle against complexity in the software's functional specification. You must also ensure that the specification of the software meets the requirements of your business – whether the software is for internal use or external sale, the software is a means to an end, not an end in itself. You must also champion the role of the software users, whether they be internal staff within your organization or your customers' staff. In addition to this role in determining the functional specification, you have an even heavier responsibility in ensuring that the non-functional characteristics of the software meet the needs of your business . . .

Ensure that the architecture of the software has the properties your business needs

How easy is it to modify the functionality of the software? How easy is it to port the software to a different operating system? How easy is it to interface the software to other pieces of software on the same or different computers? How easy is it for customers to customize the software? How easy is it to scale the software so that it can handle more users or more data? Depending on the purpose of the software, some or all of these may be very good questions – so ask them! It is important for managers to realize that none of the desirable 'ilities' (portability, flexibility, scalability, etc.) will happen by accident; they happen because the software was designed specifically to provide such properties. IT staff tend to be very focused on delivering an initial capability and often give too little attention to how the software will become a long-term part of your business. The way the software is structured (its *architecture*) will determine the answers to the questions I have posed. You should never need to know about the detailed lines of code within a software system, but you need to ask the right questions to ensure that the architecture is appropriate to your business needs.

Be flexible in adapting business processes to better suit off-the-shelf software

This point appears to rather contradict the previous point. The truth is that many off-the-shelf packages impose severe constraints on the business processes they support. This means that if you want to make the savings from using off-the-shelf software, you have got to be willing to accept the constraints that imposes on your business requirements.

Ensure that appropriate development processes are put in place

What development processes am I thinking about? I am principally talking about the things that IT staff typically know they do badly. The sorts of areas that many IT staff know they are not to be trusted with are:

- testing;
- documentation;
- coding standards;
- code reviews.

And the greatest of these is testing. I strongly advise that you ask early in a project what the test plan is, and ensure that there is adequate time and resource to do it properly. While all competent IT staff will want to test their own code, there is no substitute for energetic, independent software testing.

Managing creative types: how to herd cats

It is easy to parody the personality traits of creative people. Words such as arrogant, petulant, insecure, socially inept, unconventional and prima donna probably spring to mind. Let's look beyond the stereotypes to see what makes creative people tick, and see what management techniques can be successfully deployed on such staff.

The fear of losing the muse

Most creative people do not know 'how they do it'. As a consequence, most creative people worry or, to be more precise, are terrified that their creative ability will desert them. How do you manage this fear in your creative staff? The first thing to do is to create a culture that gives creative people a feeling of security. The best way to show this is by handling creative staff sensitively when their creativity temporarily deserts them. There are some well-proven techniques to deploy:

- Reassure the person that this is a perfectly normal situation.
- Remove deadline pressure.
- Keep the person very busy on routine work – the busier a person is, the more likely they are to regain their creativity.

Creativity often requires obsession

Creativity often requires obsession

Many creative people need to become totally obsessed by a task in order to be creative. If you manage to stop them being obsessive, they will lose their creativity. This means that you need to manage the effects that their obsession causes, but you cannot remove the root cause of the problem. It is important to distinguish the problems that are an inherent part of creativity (which you can do little or nothing about) from those that just happen to be related to creativity (which you can tackle).

The rules don't apply to me

Oh yes they do! This is one of those traits that is related to creativity that you can tackle. I would recommend that you will probably have to be a bit more tolerant of creative staff not sticking to the rules. For example, I have refrained from formally disciplining creative staff when I might have started disciplinary proceedings against a less creative staff member – because obsession does make creative staff more forgetful. However, in the final analysis, there is no reason why creative people should be allowed to get away with not obeying important rules and processes – like filling their time sheets in. A related but subtly different problem relates to individuality.

Creative personalities often do not obey behavioural norms

In many areas such as dress, behaviour and personal hygiene, creative people often stray well outside the norms expected of staff. As long as the individuality is not offensive to other staff I would recommend that you be as tolerant as your organization allows. Having to ask a staff member to wash more frequently is definitely one of the more embarrassing tasks that a manager has to face – and you do have to face it.

Lethargy often precedes creativity

Creative staff often suffer from a form of torpor before they embark on a creative task. This is perfectly normal and there is no harm in gently cajoling creative staff to try starting the task.

Creative staff tend to be very sensitive to their work environment

Creative people usually need to achieve an almost trance-like state of concentration, which psychologists refer to as 'flow'. External distractions can easily prevent the attainment of flow. For this reason, creativity and open-plan offices tend to be incompatible. For some creative staff, listening to music on headphones can help. But this is an area where you may need to be creative in your management approach. Working from home or the provision of study rooms may be the answer. Alternatively you may need to reorganize your open-plan accommodation so that those needing quiet are put close together.

They are out to get me

Not all creative people are paranoid, but it appears to me that paranoia is more common among creative people than in the population as a whole. Paranoid types need regular desensitizing by talking out their irrational fears with them.

Many creative people crave appreciation

It is important to recognize this trait when it is present, or you risk demotivating a creative staff member. It is also important because it provides opportunities for managing creative staff. Sometimes flattery will get you what you want. It can also be possible to sell a job to a creative person by telling them a task has a high profile, and will get them a lot of credit.

Consultants

There is a very narrow dividing line between consultants and some subcontractors. Here my definition of a consultant is someone who gives advice as opposed to someone who rolls their sleeves up and gets their hands dirty doing the real 'work'. I think that this definition points to one of the negative perceptions about consultants. The old saying 'those who can, do, those who can't, teach' is rephrased in many people's minds as 'those who can, do, those who can't, consult'. This is a very sensitive issue with some consultants. My perception is that it tends to be the best consultants that worry about this aspect of their work. One of the very best consultants I have worked with told me the following joke:

Question: What is the definition of a consultant?

Answer: Someone who knows over a hundred ways to make love, but is still a virgin.

It is worth being aware of the potential sensitivity about this issue for consultants, because you mention it to a consultant at your peril.

There are a number of very strong traits that most consultants share. Understanding these traits can be very useful in helping you manage consultants. In this section I will deal with two different types of interaction you may have with consultants: first, the consultants you or your organization hire to advise you and, second, the situation where you manage consultants who you sell out to do consultancy for your customers.

Consultants tend to have the mentality of gunslingers

It is important that you do not forget that consultants are hired guns. You can buy their professionalism, but you seldom buy their loyalty. A consequence of this is that consultants you hire need to be very tightly managed. You may manage your own staff in a 'hands-off' manner and because of their loyalty to the team/organization, and their membership of the team culture, they will not abuse the lack of overt management control. With consultants that you hire, you will do best if you explicitly set the parameters within which they work. If on the other hand your business is selling consultancy, and the consultants work for you, then you need to be aware that the gunslinger mentality does not naturally produce team players, and many consultants are essentially loners who may well put their own interests above the interests of the team. I have found one excellent way to create loyalty from consultants. Most consultants fear that their expertise will get out of date, and that the organization they work for will milk them for the maximum revenue that their current knowledge can generate, and will then spit them out when their expertise is out of date. If you can offer the consultants in your team the chance to generate new skills, it is much more likely that your consultants will remain loyal to your team.

Consultants tend to be competitive personalities

Much of the training for consultants is very competitive. For example, many management consultants have done MBAs, and many MBA courses are modelled on the highly competitive MBA course structure at Harvard. In addition, many consultancy companies have competitive cultures that are modelled in some way on the culture pioneered by the father of modern consulting companies – McKinsey. It would be too strong to say that all consultants are competitive, but it is a sufficiently marked trait to be worth being aware of. A side effect of the competitive natures of consultants and consulting firms is that many consultants work very long hours indeed. This means that many consultants work under very high pressure and this can make them somewhat intolerant personalities.

Consultants tend to be very aware of their remuneration

Consultancy is one of the best-paid professions. Unfortunately, combined with competitiveness and weak team-playing skills, this produces many consultants who are very focused on the amount of money they personally earn. There is almost no way a manager of consultants can avoid being sucked into highly aggressive salary negotiations, and few of the techniques that can be applied to staff to moderate their salary aspirations will work. This is one of the main reasons why staff turnover among consultants is so high, and is the main reason why consulting is one of the few professions where the top staff tend to earn salaries similar to what a poacher would pay. One technique that is worth considering is the use of non-monetary rewards. Perks and visible signs of status are often an area where a poacher will not want to match what a consultant already enjoys, for fear of opening the floodgates to dissatisfaction from the poacher's existing consultants, and this can give you a powerful argument for persuading your consultants to stay with you.

Consultants tend to intellectualize rather than empathize

Consultants tend to be analytical personalities who pride themselves on being people who can understand complex problems and who can see how those problems can be solved. Following the advice of a consultant can often cause pain and grief to some of your existing staff. Consultants will often not be very concerned about the pain their advice might cause, and this can cause tensions between consultants and the staff in the organizations they are advising.

The points above address the personal traits and personal behaviours of consultants. The following points look at some characteristics of consultants' professional behaviour.

Beware of consultants telling you what you want to hear

Telling the customer what they want to hear is the oldest trick in the consulting book. The only reason for repeating such a well-known property of consultants is that I see it happening time and time again. The next property of consultancy is almost as well known.

It is better business to tell customers good news than bad news

Just imagine a marketing consultant is brought in to advise on the marketing of a particular product, and finds that the product is almost bound to fail to be profitable. What do you think are the chances that the consultant tells the client that the product is a likely dud? This situation also occurs in many insidious ways with consultants often glossing over fundamental problems that they do not think their customers want to hear about.

Beware of becoming dependent on consultants

It is very easy for one consultancy contract to lead seamlessly into the next. You cannot expect a consultant to tell you that their advice is no longer needed; it is your responsibility to decide when paying for a consultant's advice is no longer cost-effective.

Beware of receiving 'one size fits all' advice

Many consultancy firms seek to maximize their profitability by commoditizing their service. They do this by addressing a particular range of problems and training their consultants to pigeonhole the customer's problem into one of a limited number of problem types, each of which has a standard solution. By doing this they can deskill the consultant's job by training their consultants in a standardized method. They can also increase their consultants' productivity by producing reports that contain large amounts of pre-written material. It is your job to ensure that your consultants give advice that is fully relevant to your particular situation. If you are unsure that a consultant could recognize the uniqueness of your situation, it is worth considering dispensing with their services.

Beware of advice based on a flawed method

Another approach to offering a commoditized consultancy service is to offer consultancy based on some trendy structured method. In such a situation, any limitations in the method (and all methods have limitations) can lead to inaccurate advice. The best consultancy comes from the best consultants – if you have bought the services of a well-trained monkey then you only have yourself to blame.

Beware of 'bait and switch'

Given the last two points about how consultancy firms can commoditize their services, it is not surprising that the 'bait and switch' technique is widespread in the consultancy business. This involves using the best consultants to win a contract, and then using second-rate consultants to service the contract.

Having given consultants a pretty hard time in this section, I would like to say a few words in their defence. There is nothing more depressing than working for a client who has brought in consultants just to justify what they wanted to do anyway. In particular, being brought in to recommend staff cuts has to be one of the most soul-destroying jobs in the world. Working for a client who manages you strongly and genuinely wants insight into their problems is a delight. In short, clients get the consultants they deserve.

Sales people

There are many similarities between the characteristics of sales people and those of consultants. They both tend to be poor team players; they both display a 'hired gun' mentality; they both tend to be motivated by money; they both tend to be very competitive; they both tend to be driven personalities; they both tend to allow integrity to sometimes take a back seat; and they both tend to work very long hours. There is one major difference between consultants and sales people, which is that consultants tend to be highly analytical and rational, whereas sales people tend not to be.

There are a few strong distinguishing characteristics of sales people, as described below.

Sales people are hunters

Sales people are hunters

The really good sales people enjoy chasing their quarry, and delight in the kill. Once they have begun to stalk their prey, they can find it very hard to abandon the hunt. It is important to recognize this quality if you manage sales people because a lot of them will be willing to do unreasonable things to clinch a deal. The sorts of problem that you may encounter are:

- offering too large a discount on the price;
- making unrealistic promises, such as an impossible delivery time;
- offering too many, or impossible, changes to the standard product offering;
- offering too many sweeteners, such as free advice;
- overselling the capabilities of the product.

It is your job as the manager to set the precise parameters under which your sales people operate, and to exercise discipline when (not if) those parameters are breached.

Sales people are not team players

Sales people often do not have a good relationship with product/service delivery staff. Sales people feel, with some justification, that they understand the customer better than the 'back-room' boys; that the value of their views of how the product/service should be developed to make it more saleable are not properly recognized; that they are the 'front line' of the organization and that everyone else should realize that they are only there to support them; and that everyone else in the organization fails to display a proper 'can do' attitude.

On the other hand, the staff back at base think, with some justification, that the sales people do not understand the complexity and professionalism needed to deliver a quality product or service; they resent being asked to meet impossible deadlines or compromise the quality of the product or service offering; they resent the fact that sales people do not understand the nature of the product/service and ask for features that are not consistent with the product/service ethos; they think that sales people try to keep them away from the customers; and most irritating of all that they have to work their (expletive deleted) off to earn the sales people their bonuses.

Sales people are quick to blame others

I have no idea why this tends to be the case, but from my observations it is a very marked behavioural trait in sales people.

Most sales people expect to work in a bonus culture

If you are a manager who thinks that bonuses are a very crude way to motivate staff, and who uses bonuses sparingly as a motivational aid, you need to be aware of the fact that bonuses are the norm for motivating sales people. As always it is essential to set the parameters of bonuses very carefully. For example, if a bonus is completely based on volume of business then sales people will not be motivated to push for the highest possible price; consequently, it is usually necessary to base bonuses on margins as well as volume.

Managing support staff

If you are thinking 'but I manage support staff in exactly the same way as all other team members' then award yourself a gold star for good management and skip this section. The reason I am including this section is because many managers find it difficult to manage staff whose educational and professional backgrounds are often very different from themselves. If, like me, you find this difficult, I can offer the following advice:

> *Lack of academic qualifications does not imply a lack of common sense.*

I sometimes think that the most qualified people are often the most lacking in common sense. Common sense and enthusiasm are two key qualities to look for in support staff.

It is reasonable to insist that support staff offer a very reliable service

The key to good support is its reliability. It is not acceptable if your team members feel that they have to constantly check up on support staff, rather than trusting them to get on with it.

You may need to train your team how to get the best out of support staff

Do not expect that your team members will naturally know how to use support staff to best effect. Some common misconceptions are:

- all support staff are idiots;
- all support staff are as knowledgeable as the people they support;
- all support staff are mind-readers;
- all support staff are too busy to help me;
- my job is the most urgent one.

The knack is knowing how much detail and background information you need to give a particular support person, and whether it needs to be written down or can be given verbally. Some support staff can work with a less than precise specification of a task, while others will need a fair amount of detail spelling out. It is also important to let the support staff know the deadlines for the work, and how the work relates to their other priorities.

Investing in training support staff can pay great dividends

Many support staff have never been told how to give good customer service. For example, many support staff have never been told the importance of giving the people they support feedback on the progress of a task and warning them in good time of any likely delays. In addition, the increasing use of computing technology in the workplace means you will have to invest in keeping support staff's skills up to date.

Insist that support staff be treated with respect

Some people will treat support staff like servants, without consideration or courtesy. Make sure that you let the team know that such behaviour is unacceptable. I went so far as to order the support staff to report the names of discourteous staff to me; I then made it clear to the rude staff that unless they mended their ways they would have support withdrawn from them. Politeness does not, however, mean that the team should tolerate sloppy service. If support is not totally reliable then support staff should be politely, but firmly, made aware that they have let a team member down.

Summary

You must understand what your experts are telling you. Insist that issues be explained to you in a way that you can understand. Keep asking questions until you do understand.

Beware of experts who:

- advocate particular solutions;
- say that something is impossible;
- seek to make you dependent on their continued advice.

When dealing with lawyers, remember that they tend to be risk-averse, hate moving quickly and like a good argument (preferably in court).

When dealing with IT staff, remember that software is not like traditional engineering disciplines. Estimating software projects is a black art, largely based on comparison with past projects, although one useful technique is to redo your estimates about a third of the way through the project.

Most software projects fail for reasons that are within management's control:

- inadequate requirements;
- poor consideration of the users' view of the software;
- too much complexity in the software's specification;
- unrealistic deadlines;
- management's failure to confront problems because they feel they are not qualified to intervene.

You have other key roles in managing software projects:

- ensuring that the non-functional properties of the software are addressed by the system architecture;
- ensuring that there are adequate processes for testing, code management, documentation, coding standards and code reviews.

When dealing with creative types, you must remember that many of them fear the loss of their creativity and will need continuous reassurance. Creative people often have to be obsessive in order to be creative, and you will need to decide how tolerant you will be of their obsessions, and other unattractive behavioural traits.

Consultants tend to have a gunslinger mentality. Many will not be team players. They will often be very self-centred and focused on money.

Sales people have many of the same characteristics as consultants. You need to remember that they are hunters. They will usually demand financial bonuses and will react very crudely to any financial incentives you set – so set them very carefully.

You should insist that support staff give highly reliable service. Any lack of qualifications does not imply a lack of common sense. You may well need to train your team in how to get the best out of their support staff.

CHAPTER 5

Organizing your team

Organizing yourself

The principles of time management are well known to most of us and, if not, there are many good books on the subject. However well the techniques of good time management work for you, I would give the following words of warning:

> *No matter how well you manage your time, you cannot do everything you want to do.*

This means that you must employ techniques to actually reduce the amount of work that you do, such as:

- delegation;
- reducing your level of perfectionism on appropriate tasks;
- dropping low-priority tasks.

Before looking at team organization I will say a few words on the second and third items on the list above.

Reducing your level of perfectionism on appropriate tasks

I have seen a number of managers work themselves into the ground because they had no notion of doing a job *well enough*. Put bluntly, a lot of the work you will spend your time doing is not vitally important to the future of the team. You need to discipline yourself to identify work that can be done less well and then ruthlessly limit the amount of time you put into such tasks.

Dropping low-priority tasks

I once conducted an experiment: I was getting buried by the volume of emails from other parts of my organization demanding answers of various kinds. I ignored them all and waited to see how many people chased me. Approximately 90 per cent never chased me. Of the remaining 10 per cent I replied as briefly as possible to about 80 per cent and then dealt diligently with the remaining 20 per cent I thought important. Result: I dealt with about 2 per cent diligently.

For fear of incriminating myself further I will not go on to describe other experiments I conducted into which jobs I found that I could ignore without getting into trouble. I am not recommending that you copy my somewhat irresponsible behaviour; the reason for describing these experiments is that I would suggest you think carefully about your priorities and consider whether some of your lower-priority jobs can be left undone so that you can give more time to the really important jobs.

One aspect of identifying which tasks cannot be dropped safely is to be aware of which tasks your boss is particularly interested in. Being brutally cynical, it is worth finding out which tasks you do could impact on your boss's bonus, because you drop those at your peril!

Management tasks

Before looking at possible ways of organizing your team it is worth reviewing a typical list of the major tasks the average manager has to do:

- firefighting – people queuing up to ask for your help in resolving problems;

- business strategy formulation;
- staff management issues (such as staff appraisals and pay setting);
- staff and other resource allocation;
- operations management (finance, accommodation and all the other niff, naff and trivia of running a team);
- interfacing with the rest of the organization (both routine and special initiatives);
- head of state (someone needs to wheel the boss out);
- emissary (setting up links to other groups inside and outside the organization);
- salesperson;
- negotiator;
- schmoozing with customers;
- reviewing the outputs of the team.

Delegating responsibilities

The first thing to stress is that the organization of your team has to be built around the skills of the staff you have or the staff you can recruit. The approach of designing an idealized team structure, and then trying to fill all the posts within that structure, can only work if the team is large enough that you are likely to find enough staff with the requisite skills. Given that this book is aimed at the lowest level of managers in an organization, you will do much better to build a team structure around the people you have to hand.

You need to focus on the fact that you will only have a limited number of staff who can lead a project or task and be relied on to bring it in successfully. Say you have five such staff, then you can only do five things really well – so make sure those five staff are working on the five most important roles. You will then have to manage the fact that other tasks are quite likely not to run smoothly.

Before discussing which jobs you may choose to delegate, it is important to remind you that the main purpose of delegating is to reduce your workload. There is absolutely no point in delegating a task and then continuing to give it the same level of attention as you would if you were doing the job yourself. Every task needs one person to worry about it. If you are delegating a task to someone who will not worry about it then you are delegating it to the wrong person. It is no use at all if you feel you need to constantly check that the task is being done properly. This does not mean that you maintain no visibility of the task, but you must agree up front how you are going to maintain an appropriate level of visibility, and then let the person get on with it.

The obvious roles you can delegate are those of routine personnel management and operations management. Of these two roles the more important to delegate is the operations management because it is so time-consuming and stressful. In addition the type of personality that makes for a good leader is frequently not the right person to handle the day-to-day detailed operations of the team. You can delegate operations management at a number of levels. At one extreme you can pass off most of the responsibilities to a professional business administrator. At the other extreme you can retain the major responsibilities and have a reliable office assistant to execute the bulk of the routine duties.

If you are not good at interpersonal relationships then I strongly suggest that you try to find someone to delegate personnel management to. Even if you do not feel the need to delegate many of these responsibilities there is an advantage in having someone within your team who regularly talks to staff about their concerns. Such a person can be used as an intermediary between the staff and yourself. No matter how good you are at interpersonal relationships you will always be the boss, and staff will find it less easy to be totally open with you than they would with an independent person. The independent person can then approach you on a specific individual's behalf or can raise an issue of 'general concern' without identifying anyone in particular. I have used such a system for many years and it has always worked extremely well. If your organization has a good personnel department or good trades union representatives, they can fulfil a similar role.

If you are delegating some of your responsibilities you will want to consider having a group of trusted lieutenants who act as a small board with yourself as chairperson/chief executive. If you have the right people, who get on well together, this can work wonderfully. However, if there is no group with the right chemistry then it is better to act alone as the leader figure.

You will probably be required to nominate a deputy or deputies. There are two distinct ways of handling this. The deputy can be used solely to deputize in your absence, with the expectation that they will try not to make major decisions in your absence. The other way is to have your deputy empowered at all times and you ensure they are kept in the picture so that they can make real decisions. Which method you choose will depend on how much you trust, and how well you can work with, your deputy.

If you have appropriate staff it can be useful to have members of the team working directly for you, even if only for part of their time. Such staff could act as general assistants to you or they could do particular projects on your behalf, such as implementing one of the initiatives dreamed up by head office. This approach has three beneficial effects: first, it will reduce the load on you; second, it can be useful for developing the careers of the staff who work for you; and, last, the staff who work directly for you can help you understand what issues the members of the team are worrying about.

Depending on the size of your team you may need to introduce a level of management between yourself and the rest of the team. If you have to do this you are moving away from the type of manager this book is particularly targeted at. There is, however, a limit to the size of team you can manage in a totally flat hierarchy.

One area that is worthy of careful thought is the level of administrative support you put into your team. One extreme position is to hire more value-creating staff and make them do their own photocopying, travel arrangements and the like. The other extreme view is that it is crazy to have highly paid staff doing menial tasks. My own view is that excellent support is very cost-effective, but poor support is worse than useless.

Using consultants

We have all seen organizations that become overly dependent on management consultants. There are, however, times when hiring someone from outside your team is appropriate:

- When an outside viewpoint is needed. You and your team may well be basing your decisions on implicit assumptions that an outsider can challenge. Outsiders will also be dispassionate, which can help counteract the passion in yourself and the team.
- When you want to bring in a particular skill on a temporary basis. For example, if you are trying to build a new business opportunity in a market area that is new to your team, it can be useful to hire marketing and sales consultants with experience in the new market area, until it is clear

whether that opportunity is, or is not, going to be successful.

Summary

The way you delegate responsibilities is one of the principal techniques you can use to control your workload. It is also a way of covering for areas that you are weak in.

There is no single right way to organize your team. This chapter gives a range of techniques that can be used *if, and only if, you have the right staff available in your team to delegate the responsibilities to* – you have to work with the staff you have available.

CHAPTER 6

Business management

Even if you do not have explicit financial responsibility for the profit and loss of your team, it is likely that you have significant control over how your team delivers value to its customers and how the team's offerings to its customers will develop in the future. Although you are unlikely to manage the stark life or death issues that an entrepreneur faces, you are likely to need many of the fundamental skills of a business person. The large number of basic business mistakes I have seen managers make over the years seems to indicate that the basics of business management are either not widely understood or that they are not widely applied. Consequently, I felt that a chapter devoted to the basics of business management was worth including.

Back to basics

Marketing has a slightly shifty image, but the fundamentals of marketing are the basics of your team's business proposition:

- What products and services do you sell now and what will you sell in the future?
- Who are your target customers?
- Who are your competitors and how do they compete with your business?

- How do you want your customers to perceive your products and services?
- How do you create the right perception in potential customers' minds?
- How will your customers differentiate your products and services from those of your competitors?
- How do you price your services?
- How do your customers find out about your product and service offerings?

You then have to sell your services, build a loyal customer base, maintain high levels of customer satisfaction, spot changes in the market that could put you out of business, react to those changes, manage major business risks . . . easy, huh!

Before you go getting all depressed, it is worth remembering you are not trying to start a business from scratch – you probably already have a viable business. This chapter will concentrate on how you can sharpen up your business rather than on creating a new business from scratch.

Product positioning and marketing

There are a few key principles you need to be aware of. The first is counter-intuitive:

The smaller, more focused your target market is, the easier it is to market your products and services

There is an understandable tendency to make your products and services suitable for as large a potential market as possible. In reality, the more clearly you differentiate your product so that it more precisely fits the needs of a specific market segment, the easier your products and services will be to sell, and the easier you will be able to defend your market from competitors. A great advantage of this approach is that it can help avoid getting into price wars with competitors. In this way, a strong, differentiated market position is a good way to preserve healthy margins.

Customers' perceptions of your products and services will be very simplistic and can usually be expressed in a few simple words or phrases

The first thing to notice here is that it is the customers' *perceptions* that matter, not the reality of your products and services. It is no use complaining that the customers have got the wrong perceptions; it is your actions, or inactions, that have allowed the wrong perceptions to take hold, and it is your job to change those perceptions.

Second, you need to ensure that you plan which simple words and phrases you want to jump into your customers' minds and plan your products, services, advertising and public relations to reinforce a simple, understandable positioning of your products and services. Possibly the commonest fault is to base your business on too complex a product positioning.

Formulate your product positioning on benefits you offer customers, not the features of your products and services

A very common mistake! Try not to position your product on its technical features; position it on what benefits it offers the customer. Some features are closely related to benefits: for example, a car engine with 16 valves is probably more powerful than an 8-valve engine of similar capacity; but it is usually best to find out what the customer values and position your product as satisfying that need. For example, the Japanese success in car manufacture was largely based on satisfying customers' desire for highly reliable vehicles. Another example from the car industry is that Volvo built its market positioning largely based on the safety of its cars.

When positioning your products and services, think about them from the customers' viewpoint

Remember that a benefit is some attribute of your products and services that *customers* value. Management gurus go on, and on, about getting close to your customer, and when it comes to product positioning they are absolutely right. A story I heard that illustrated this point very well was about a washing machine repair organization that was investing very heavily in improving the response time of their washing machine repair engineers. Then someone from marketing sent out a questionnaire to their customers that showed the primary cause of dissatisfaction was repairmen not turning up on time, and not phoning to say they were going to be late.

Brand names are really important

Given the simplicity of customers' perceptions, the names you give your products and services are really important. Brand names encapsulate the trust that customers perceive in your products and services. At your level of the organization you may well not be in the business of registering trademarks; however, it may well be worth getting a check done that any names you use do not infringe existing registered trademarks or clash with existing Internet domain names.

An issue you need to consider is the extent to which you concentrate the brand names on your products and services, and the extent to which you want to build up a reputation in the team's name. Generally speaking I would discourage building up a team brand name, if only because organizations reorganize so frequently that your team's name will probably not last very long.

Beware of stretching a brand name

Brand stretching, also called line extension, is when you use a successful brand name to try to sell a new product or service. You will need to read a marketing book to fully understand how dangerous brand stretching can be; however, the simplest explanation is that it can break the fundamental principle of narrowly focusing your product and service positioning.

Brand stretching is a very common mistake because it is a very sound business practice to use your existing products and services as a basis for developing new business opportunities. For example, you may wish to develop a new product that is similar to one of your existing products and that will appeal to a new set of customers. In such circumstances it is very attractive to use the reputation of your existing product to give 'instant credibility' to your new offering. In some circumstances it can be best to create a new product identity – you need to decide if the advantage to the new product is worth the risk to the current value of the brand name.

Honesty is an effective marketing tool

By narrowly focusing your products and services you are creating strong positive differentiators from your competitors. It will also mean clearly acknowledging that for many customers yours is the wrong product or service. Openly acknowledging the limitations of your products and services means that you will get fewer enquiries from customers who should not buy your offering; and it also increases the credibility of your positive claims.

Beware of price reductions as a promotional tool

It is all too easy to get fixated on price as the principal means of increasing your volume of business. If your business is not well differentiated from your competitors then price may indeed be the key factor that influences your customers. If price is not the key factor in a customer's decision to purchase your products and services then think carefully before offering to reduce your margins.

Be bold! It's the only safe thing to do

Given the simplicity of customers' perceptions, and the difficulty of getting people's attention, a timid marketing strategy is likely to be useless.

Read a good marketing book

My own personal favourites can be found in the 'Suggested reading' section at the end of this chapter.

Use standard business planning techniques, but do not let them distract you from the basics

There are many standard textbooks that cover the material taught in a typical MBA course. I would suggest that you read at least one of them so that you are aware of standard business planning techniques such as SWOT (Strengths, Weaknesses, Opportunities, Threats) analysis and the variants of product grids, such as the Boston Matrix. My view is that almost any structured form of analysis will give you insight into your business, but it is all too easy to just apply the standard techniques and to avoid the really deep analysis of product positioning and marketing that is so important to a successful business.

Strategy and planning

This section could have been subtitled 'Get Lucky'. If you look back at the successful things you have been involved in, how many of them were the result of deliberate planning and how many were the result of a happy coincidence of the right thing, in the right place, at the right time? It is my thesis that almost all detailed planning quickly becomes invalidated by unpredictable events. Whereas I view long-range *planning* as a generally futile activity, I believe that the creation of a long-term *strategy* can be of great value.

What is the value of a long-term strategy? In a nutshell it helps you react intelligently to emerging circumstances, so that you can instantly recognize that lucky coincidence of events that presents a significant opportunity to the business. One example might be that you have decided that strategically you need to extend the core capabilities of your business to include a particular new capability; if a business opportunity then comes up that would fund you to build up that new capability, you will probably jump at that opportunity. Another example might be that you decide strategically that you want to break into a new niche market segment; then, if you get an opportunity that would create a great reference customer in that niche market, you would probably go all out for that opportunity. Luck is often a matter of recognizing the lucky circumstance, and not allowing it to pass you by.

Designing a good strategy is a creative activity and experienced managers tend to be much better at it than inexperienced ones. One way to learn the technique is to evaluate each new opportunity that emerges from a strategic viewpoint. If your existing strategy does not help you evaluate the opportunity then consider what aspect you could add to your strategy that would help you evaluate it. In this way a strategy can grow with time.

Strategies tend to be better at evaluating opportunities than they are at recognizing and responding to threats. One of your key roles as the business leader is to ensure the long-term survival of your team's business. To do this you need to spot those changes to the external environment in which your team operates that pose a fundamental threat to your team's existence. The two greatest threats are a change in the political structure of your organization and a change in the nature of the market in which you sell your products and services – be that inside or outside your organization.

I do not intend to say anything about monitoring the politics inside your organization. You will have to decide the extent to which an understanding of those politics enables you to adjust your strategy accordingly. My somewhat naive view is that in most circumstances the best defence against such politics is to build a strong business of significant value to your organization.

Spotting potentially disruptive changes in your markets can only be done by maintaining a broad understanding of market trends. This tends to be best done by general reading in the mainstream and trade press. If you are an enthusiast for your business area then this is something you probably do anyway. If you are not an enthusiast then you need to create a market-watching activity within your team and listen to their analysis of potentially disruptive changes. Even if you do your own market-watching it will often benefit you to discuss market trends with other market watchers in your team. Many teams/businesses go out of business because they do not react fast enough to a disruptive change in their markets – you ignore market watching at your peril!

Writing a business strategy

What are the contents of a business strategy? I suggest you consider your strategy under six interrelated headings: product positioning; team capabilities; team organization and processes; the external environment; links to the external environment; and a risk analysis. I also suggest that you focus only on the *major changes* under these headings. Another important rule of management is:

You can only do a few things well.

I have already made the point that your products and services can only be differentiated on a few things you do much better than your competitors. It also applies to the challenges you set yourself in your strategy; you can only make a few changes at any one time. The good news is that if you write down a realistic business strategy it will usually fit on one or two pages.

Product positioning

This describes major changes you would like to develop in your product and service positioning. This could be an enhancement or evolution of the competitive differentiators of your current products and services. It could be a new product or service offering that builds closely on one of your existing offerings. Or, rarely, it could be a radically new offering that your current expertise allows you to contemplate.

What major changes in your customer base are you going to pursue? This could be a way of growing your existing customer base, for example by reducing prices, or increasing promotion, or enhancing your channels to market. Or by selling an existing service to new types of customers. Or by adapting an existing product or service to attract a new type of customer.

The previous two paragraphs both concentrate on growth. Equally important is to identify which areas are going to be downgraded or closed down.

Team capabilities

How do you want to change your team's *core competencies*? (There's that strange dialect *management-speak* again.) Core competencies just refer to the areas of knowledge and expertise that are available within your team. For example, an architectural practice might have considerable knowledge and expertise in the design of novel glass structures. Another example might be that a software design firm is expert in designing signalling systems for the railways. An example of a change in team capabilities might be for the software design firm to exploit its links with the railway industry to develop a capability in information system design – such as software that links sensor data into customer information systems displayed on platforms.

Team organization and processes

The different aspects of the business strategy are all interrelated. You may identify a change in organization or process as the best way to achieve some other element of the strategy. Examples might be the appointment of account managers, or a process for quickly answering customer complaints.

The external environment

What major changes are there external to your organization that might impact on your business in the market? These could include technology, competitors, regulatory and legal issues, mergers and acquisitions, and your major customers.

As mentioned earlier, it is this area that must be *constantly* watched for changes that could disrupt your team. Disruptive changes can seldom be predicted; the trick is to spot them, and react to them, before your existing, or new, competitors do.

Links to the external environment

This is the topic a lot of managers miss. Under this heading you should think about the following areas:

- Which other organizations, or other parts of your own organization, could you form common cause with? Other organizations could include suppliers, collaborators, partners and trade associations.
- External channels you use to sell your products and services.
- Your sources of external intelligence. These include publications, consultants' reports, market research (published, commissioned or directly obtained by questionnaires),

networking using your team's contacts, attendance at exhibitions, conferences, seminars and the like, and company databases.

- Links to the press, advertising, and links to your organization's PR and advertising departments.

Risk analysis

The changes your strategy proposes are themselves a risk. It is very motivating to have bold objectives in a strategy, but what is the downside if you fail to achieve your objectives? In extremis your strategy could be 'betting the team' and failure could mean the end of the team. If the business situation is desperate then desperate measures may be the only option. This section of the strategy should compare the risks and benefits of the strategy, and check they are commensurate.

Reacting to threats and opportunities

The main reason for not reacting fast is in your head

Many management gurus have already highlighted the rapidly rising pace of business. Product cycles are reducing, customer aspirations are rising, and technology changes are destabilizing previously stable businesses. The gurus then draw the obvious conclusion that organizations that are quick on their feet have a massive advantage. I will argue in a later chapter that managers usually have much greater power than they are granted explicitly by their organizations. So, a new opportunity or threat has been identified – can you react immediately to it? Reacting will inevitably create knock-on problems; key staff may have to be moved or existing programmes de-emphasized or even abandoned. In short, reacting involves you in a lot of work. It is all too easy to find reasons why 'the system' is stopping you from reacting, when in reality the problems are in your head.

You often need to overreact to bad news

When things go wrong it is very easy to underestimate how fast things will deteriorate. Always bear in mind that an over-reaction seldom does any harm, but not reacting fast enough, or strongly enough, can often do irreparable damage.

You often need to overreact to bad news

If you need to be ruthless, do not use half measures

There will inevitably be times when you have to make a ruthless move. In these circumstances do not be half-hearted. Go in as hard and fast as you can, and when you have your opponent down – kick them! If it is dog eat dog, it is your duty to make sure you do the eating.

Hopefully this advice will make you think long and hard before you decide on a ruthless course of action. I am pointing out that leaving a wounded enemy is a very dangerous thing to do. However, even if you defeat your opponent completely, they may have a chance at some later date to get even. For this reason it is important to play hard but fair. Your opponents may forgive you for winning a fair fight, but if you play dirty you can expect your opponent to look for every opportunity for 'payback'.

Managing your business processes

Carefully select your control measures

In *management-speak* this is the tight aspect of a *loose/tight* system. It is usually best to select only a few aspects of your business you keep very tight control over. Possible examples are running costs, project reviews and capital expenditure. There is no magic recipe here; you need to select controls that suit your business, your own organization's controls, the culture . . . in short, everything. You need to be aware of the fact that your staff will respond very literally to the tight processes, which can cause unforeseen undesirable consequences. As an example, you need to set bonuses and incentives very carefully, otherwise they may have unfortunate, distorting effects on staff behaviour.

Top-down processes only work for well-defined tasks

A top-down process requires that a task be planned in detail before it is undertaken. A bottom-up process does a bit of the task and then uses what has been found out to help plan the next part of the task. Top-down tends to work when you are doing a well-understood task. Bottom-up is much more suitable when you are attempting something for the first time. Managers tend to feel much more comfortable with the predictability of top-down processes, but using them for poorly defined tasks is futile.

Processes can break down as a team grows in size

There tend to be natural discontinuities relating to team size. A team of, say, 5 people can rely largely on informal processes because everyone knows what everyone else is doing. A team of up to, say, 20–30 people can work without intermediate levels of management, with you knowing everyone and everything that is going on. Much bigger than 20–30 and you will have to structure the team so that you do not have such direct control over all the activities of the team. If your team is growing, be alert for signs that your organizational structure and processes are no longer able to cope, and redesign them.

Discontinuities in team size often coincide with other business discontinuities. For example, if one of your products or services has suddenly broken through into the mainstream market you will often have to cope with major business issues, as well as a sudden growth in the size of your team. Many small companies fail to manage such discontinuities successfully. If you work within a larger organization there should be a support structure to help your team through periods of rapid growth. In such situations designing and staffing a management structure suitable for your new size and new business opportunities should be your top priority; otherwise you and your team will run faster and faster and faster, and it is almost inevitable that the team will 'lose the plot'.

Finance, legal and negotiations

There are four areas where you need at least a minimal level of expertise – legal, regulatory, finance and negotiating.

You cannot dismiss legal and regulatory issues as someone else's problem; you need to understand any legal documents you sign, and you need to understand any possible legal risks your business is exposed to. Unfortunately I have not found a good book to recommend. I suggest you contact your legal advisers and see if they can recommend any training courses, or whether they have any written advice specific to your organization. You also need to understand regulatory issues such as health and safety, discrimination and anti-trust. Legal and regulatory issues can destroy a business or destroy your career and you must manage that risk by having enough understanding to avoid major pitfalls.

You have to understand the finances of your team or project. There are plenty of training courses on the basics of finance and it is likely that your organization can recommend an appropriate one. You need to understand the concepts that underlie the 'balance sheet' for your team's activities. Not understanding the financial status of your team is like flying a fast jet, in fog, at low level, in the mountains, *without instruments* – potentially fatal. Personally I find this aspect of a manager's job incredibly boring, but if asked if I mind doing it I would answer 'not when you consider the alternative'.

Finally, you are likely to negotiate on behalf of your team, even if it is only for resources within your organization. There are plenty of great courses on negotiation techniques – if you have not been on one, stop reading and get yourself on one now!

Know it, do it, say it

The 80:20 rule (Pareto's Law)

The 80:20 rule encapsulates the truth that many business issues are not uniformly distributed. So, for example, it is typical that 80 per cent of your revenue will come from 20 per cent of your customers; 80 per cent of the aggravation will come from 20 per cent of your customers; 20 per cent of your staff are key to 80 per cent of your business; 80 per cent of personnel management time is spent on 20 per cent of your staff. Wise managers understand Pareto's Law and adjust their priorities accordingly.

Drill more wells

It is sensible to recognize that Pareto's Law applies to new business opportunities. Typically 80 per cent fail and only 20 per cent will make money. Even within the 20 per cent that make money, Pareto's Law may well apply again, and only 20 per cent of the 20 per cent will make big bucks. With this level of failure rates you will often do better to start multiple opportunities, as cheaply as possible, and then pour resources into the ones that come up trumps.

The title of this section is based on a possibly apocryphal story about a comparison of two oil companies' exploration activities. Both companies spent similar amounts on oil exploration. One company spent a lot of money on geological surveys prior to drilling. The other company spent less time on geological surveys and spent the money saved to drill more test bores. The company that did more drilling found more oil.

Manage the downside

A side effect of *drilling more wells* is to acknowledge that most opportunities will fail, so ensure that you analyze the costs and liabilities of them failing and actively manage them so as to minimize that downside. You may find that a downside analysis is also an excellent way of selecting which opportunities not to pursue. Following this point a bit further:

Saying no is often more important than saying yes

One of the reasons for having a business strategy is to say no to an opportunity that lands in your lap. It is really hard to turn down easy business, but business that does not fit in with your strategy will stop you pursuing opportunities that do fit with your strategy – so it is not easy business, it is a distraction. Obviously this assumes that you are not desperately short of business!

Why stretch? Pick the low-lying fruit first

This is so obvious, so please explain to me why we don't do it more. Why spend huge resources on some risky venture when there is a less glamorous opportunity whose cost–benefit ratio is much better? I think the answer lies in the word *glamorous.* A related tip is:

Remember, the easiest sale is to an existing customer

Of all the forms of low-lying fruit, the one that is most often overlooked is the potential to sell additional products and services to your existing customers. You have already broken the sales barrier with your existing customers and often extra business is there for the asking.

Don't neglect your existing customers

Also remember that it is far easier to lose an existing customer than it is to find a new one; so invest in caring for your existing customers.

Avoid unpleasant surprises.

The important word here is *surprises.* When you know things are going wrong, let the customer know as soon as possible, do not just hope that things will get better . . . they usually get even worse. Customers approached in good time will usually be receptive to a sensible negotiation about managing the problem. This is a special case of a more general rule:

Honesty pays

One of the pleasures of management is that the right thing is usually the smartest thing. If your customer trusts you then everything is so much easier.

Underclaim, and overdeliver

Under pressure to win a sale or soothe an aggrieved customer there is a terrible temptation to quote the best possible delivery time or the lowest possible estimate of extra costs. Try to resist this temptation. In the long term, the smartest thing to do is to add a reasonable contingency and then come in under time and under budget. In many cases lost sales will be more than balanced out by the long-term benefits to your reputation.

Obviously, this advice is predicated on your business being well enough established to be able to afford some short-term loss of sales as an investment for long-term gain. I am sure many readers will find themselves in situations where a customer request to dance naked in the street with a rose in your teeth will be answered by the question, 'What colour rose would you like?'

Problems are often opportunities

Most customers know that their suppliers will make mistakes. A key issue for many customers is how a supplier handles a mistake. So when your team messes up you must recognize it as an opportunity to extend your relationship with that customer by showing them how well you can retrieve a situation.

Talk to the front line

The best way for you to keep your finger on the pulse of your current business is to talk to your staff who directly interact with customers. As just one example, these staff are likely to know about possibilities for selling additional products and services to your existing customers. They are also likely to be aware of what are the 'hot topics' in the customer's mind, which will be excellent indicators of emerging market trends that could well become disruptive forces, or opportunities, for your business.

Beware the limitations of analogy

One advantage an experienced manager has is the ability to say 'that will not work because I remember when we did . . .'

The danger of applying your past experience to draw analogies with a current situation is that circumstances may have changed. In my own area of information technology a common mistake is to say that 'so-and-so has never worked in the past', but computer performance has now improved to an extent where 'so-and-so' is now possible.

Beware the dangers of extrapolation

It is very easy to assume that a current trend will continue. For example, a market that has been growing at 25 per cent a year can easily lead you to unconsciously assume that the trend will continue, and when it does not you can find yourself overextended. Always be alert for the first signs that a trend is changing and be prepared to (over)react. Always consider investments in the light of the fact that trends may change.

Beware diversification

Many small teams will, in business terms, have all their eggs in one basket. In such circumstances there is a great temptation to diversify into other areas. However, diversification tends to reduce marketing focus and it is often better to stick to what you know best. The first thought for diversification should be to apply your core competencies to a new, but related, market area.

Summary

The single most important aspect of business management is to establish a *simple, clear, focused* idea of how your products and services are perceived by your customers, which clearly differentiates your products and services from those of your competitors.

You should use a business strategy to allow you to spot those opportunities that can provide a strategic advantage to your business. A good strategy will also help you identify those opportunities you should not pursue. Saying no at the right time is just as important as being a 'can do' business.

You must make the time to scan the external environment in which your business operates for the first signs of disruptive changes that could put you out of business. These could be any of a host of threats including technological changes, mergers and acquisitions creating a new competitor, and changes in regulation. When you spot such a change you must be ready to act hard and fast to counter the threat, and to turn that threat into an opportunity.

Remember Pareto's Law:

- Invest in keeping and exploiting (in the nicest possible way) the 20 per cent of your customers who give you 80 per cent of your business.
- Remember, 80 per cent of new opportunities will lose money, so manage the costs of new opportunities very tightly until it is clear they are winners.

Finally, do not ignore the unglamorous low-lying fruit. Make sure that you go for the obvious extensions to your core business first.

Suggested reading

Ries, Al and Jack Trout (1994), *The 22 Immutable Laws of Marketing: Violate Them at Your Own Risk*: New York, Harperbusiness.

A short, highly readable introduction to the basics of marketing and brands.

Ries, Al and Laura Ries (2000), *The 22 Immutable Laws of Branding*, London, HarperCollinsBusiness.

A short, highly readable introduction to brand management. Some overlap with *The 22 Immutable Laws of Marketing*.

Shell, G. Richard (2000), *Bargaining for Advantage: Negotiation Strategies for Reasonable People*: London, Penguin Books.

A very practical, comprehensive book on good negotiating tactics.

Moore, Geoffrey A. (1999), *Crossing the Chasm: Marketing and Selling High-Tech Products to Mainstream Customers*: New York, Harperbusiness.

Moore, Geoffrey A. (1997), *Inside the Tornado: Marketing Strategies from Silicon Valley's Cutting Edge*: New York, HarperCollins.

'Must reads' if you are in the high-tech industry. I think that many of the ideas are relevant for non-high-tech businesses.

CHAPTER 7

Managing your organization

A confession

Until this point in the book I think I can reasonably claim I have 'practised what I am preaching'. In this chapter I am suggesting that you 'do as I say, not as I did'. Putting a positive spin on the situation, I am offering you the hard-won experience of many a battle-scarred manager.

Managing your managers

Do not get emotional

No matter how stupid, demotivating, contradictory and small-minded you think your managers are – *STAY CALM.* If you get emotional, you are dead. The problem is that if you are good at your job you are likely to be passionate about it, and in dealing with the rest of your organization you have to be cool and cerebral.

In most organizations your bosses will be middle managers. You need to understand that middle managers inhabit a world that is considerably more surreal than any created by J.R.R. Tolkien (why do you think he called it *Middle* Earth?). Most middle managers know little more than you do about the strategic direction of your organization and spend their entire lives trying to satisfy the magic processes spun by the wizards from head office. Do not get angry with them, it is probably

Do not get emotional

not their fault. Also remember that, like most people who practise the black arts, they can be very dangerous.

Never threaten people's authority

The 'powers that be' will not accept explicit threats to their authority, so you need to achieve your objectives without any crude confrontations.

Good teams are, by their nature, threatening

One of the most depressing facts about being a small team within a larger organization is that the better your team does, the more it will threaten other people and teams in the organization. The only way to tackle this is to go beyond the mere avoidance of threatening behaviour and to actually be friendly to those who implicitly feel threatened. The easiest way to do this is to try to get them to feel part of your success. Seek advice and help from people and teams who may feel threatened.

Never, ever, threaten to resign

Just as I advise that you should not give in to threats from your key staff, I think that any sensible organization should accept your resignation. Threatening to resign is never the way to handle a conflict.

It is possible that you will be put in a position that is completely untenable, in which case you may have to resign. If you are unlucky enough to find yourself in this situation, just go quietly.

Cock-ups are more common than conspiracies

It is very easy to convince yourself that the organization is out to get you and your team. It is my experience that cock-ups are far more common than conspiracies. Communication within organizations is usually pretty awful. When you start seeing conspiracies behind every tree, it is best to go and have a chat with your boss, or whoever you think is conspiring. I suggest you go in thinking the best . . . it's probably just normal organizational incompetence!

It is also important to keep pointing out this viewpoint to your team. There are bound to be plenty of conspiracy theorists in your team. It is important that you provide a calming influence to your team, because the mood will tend to be anti-establishment. Middle managers, personnel managers, accountants, lawyers et al. tend not to be bad people; they are usually doing their best under very difficult circumstances. It is important that you try to be tolerant yourself, and try to imbue that tolerance in the team.

Do not fight battles you cannot win or are not worth the effort

Your team will tend to see every action of 'the system' as an attempt to destroy the team's value. There will occasionally be genuine threats that you have to avert by the more subtle methods I outline below. There will, however, be many issues that you either cannot win or which are not worth the effort to fight. As with so many things, there are only a few things you can do at any one time. Do not waste your, and the team's, efforts on issues that you cannot win or which are not genuinely life-threatening.

As an example, when introducing ISO 9001 quality processes into the team, my organization mandated a very unpopular standard format for official reports, and mandated that a particular word processor be used to produce them. The team unanimously wanted me to fight this proposal tooth and nail. I told them bluntly that (a) we would lose, and (b) there were more important issues to win. There were many grumbles, but my view was accepted.

The theory of 'free power'

There are a number of different ways to express this theory. The chief executive of my organization gave a definition I liked:

> *It is easier to ask for forgiveness than it is to ask for permission.*

Most organizations do not really know how much authority they have delegated to low-level managers. Many organizations help you by saying fine words about empowerment. So in many cases you can just go ahead and do things.

The main disadvantage is that most organizations default to a blame culture, so there will be no comeback if your decision turns out well, but you will get blamed if things go wrong. You have to decide if you care about being blamed. If you just want to do a good job on behalf of your team I suggest you use organizational free power a lot.

A good technique, well backed up by psychology, is to be submissive and apologetic when being blamed. It is really hard, and no fun, to beat up someone when they are grovelling.

One situation when I strongly recommend the use of organizational free power is when the organization definitely does not want to be asked to give permission. For example, if a staff member asks your permission to do something that is not covered by the rules then if it is a reasonable request just say yes. In most countries your decision will legally bind your organization, but the organization does not want to have to make a decision that may set an organization-wide precedent. In such cases, the organization will probably be much happier if you assume the local responsibility for the decision.

Find the wiggle room

Within any organizational process or instruction there is nearly always room for local 'interpretation'. Often it will be possible to show that your local interpretation is in the original spirit of the process or instruction. As an example, when I oversaw the introduction of ISO 9001 quality processes into my team, I got a copy of the actual standard and easily showed that my local interpretations of the corporate quality processes were directly supported by the ISO 9001 document. As the organization only really cared that the independent quality accreditors would not give me any non-compliances, they left me alone.

Few organizations will fire you for not doing things

In the last resort, rather than threatening to resign, you will usually get away with not carrying out instructions to the letter. Provided you do not rub your management's noses in the fact that you are being insubordinate, you will usually get away with it.

I strongly recommend that you use this technique very sparingly indeed. Although your superiors may not fire you, they are likely to be able to make life very difficult for you at some time in the future.

Ask for help

When dealing with other departments, such as personnel or finance, a good tactic is to appeal to their professional vanity by asking them how something outside the normal rules can be done. If you seek assistance from someone who has professional pride they will often tell you where the wiggle room is.

Going one step further, if you develop a good relationship with a particular person, then your dealings with that department can be transformed. One way to help develop such a relationship is to be courteous – for example by thanking someone when they have done a good job.

Tap into the support subculture

Secretaries and support staff of all kinds are a valuable source of information and help in dealing with the rest of your organization. If you extend my advice about being courteous to your team members to people outside your team then you will find it relatively easy to tap into the support subculture. You will find that stopping for a chat with secretaries and support staff is not only very interesting, it can also be very informative, and that such people often have some power to help you, and always have great power to hinder you.

Initiatives

Organizations seem very keen these days on buzzword-based initiatives. Knowledge management, quality, total quality, re-engineering, benchmarking and the like all seem to be rolled out at regular intervals. In addition, there are the annual processes such as business planning to be dealt with, which seem to change their form each year. How does one handle them?

Be first or last

There is an advantage in being first to embrace an initiative. You will get brownie points. You will also have the maximum say in setting the interpretation of the initiative. Otherwise, let the other suckers get all the bugs out and do it at the last possible moment.

Hijack the initiative

Initiatives often come with some sort of funding, even if it is only some allowance of time for you and your staff. Consider if you can use the initiative to make some change that you wanted to make anyway. As an example, many people use the introduction of quality processes to re-engineer a slicker set of procedures in the team.

The great advantage of such an approach is that the team is likely to be more motivated in implementing the initiative if there is some direct benefit to the team. It is my view that the skilful manager can turn almost all initiatives to some advantage. This avoids the difficult situation where you are trying to get the team to implement an initiative that your staff know you do not really believe in.

Use the initiative to negotiate a change in your targets

It is often possible to use an initiative to negotiate a change to your existing targets with your boss. Your boss may well accept that the new priority implied by the latest initiative means that existing priorities have to be reassessed.

Do initiatives 'well enough'

Avoid the mistake of overdoing the level of effort to implement an initiative. If you put it positively – that you are looking to get the maximum 'bangs for the buck' from the initiative – this will not be seen as a criticism of the initiative.

Your personal bonus and targets

This is a very dangerous subject. Your staff will know that you are likely to have targets to meet. They will suspect, often correctly, that these targets are very crude measures of performance, and they will suspect that you are allowing the pursuit of your bonus to unduly affect your behaviour.

Tell the team what your targets and bonuses are

There is no better way to defuse the suspicions of your team than being totally open. I also suggest that you acknowledge that the smart thing to do is to keep 'them' happy by hitting as many of the targets as possible. Although the targets are likely to be crude, it is usually possible to achieve them without doing any significant damage to other more important performance indicators. If the targets are really damaging I suggest you discuss with the team the extent to which you should balance the targets against the other more important factors – remembering that you cannot just ignore the organization's targets, no matter how stupid they are.

In Chapter 3 I recommended that you use part of your bonus to sponsor team social events – after all, it is their efforts you are being rewarded for.

Summary

The four most important messages from this chapter for the brilliant manager are:

1 Do not get emotional with your bosses. Passion is a great attribute of a leader, but a terrible way to manage the rest of your organization.

2. Use the 'free power' within the organization. It is better to apologize after the event than ask for permission beforehand.
3. Find the wiggle room within your organization's processes. Best of all, get a good working relationship with other departments in your organization, particularly finance, contracts, legal and personnel.
4. Try to hijack your organization's initiatives to implement improvements within your team.

CHAPTER 8

Key management themes

There are several key themes that underpin all of management. Some of them have been touched on in earlier chapters. This chapter brings them to the surface and looks at them as a whole.

Managing the dependencies

Although this book discusses different aspects of management in isolation, you must consider them as a whole. Your leadership style must be appropriate to the culture you are creating. The team's culture must be appropriate to the sort of business you are in, and the customers you sell products and services to. Your business must fit your team's capabilities. Your team's organization and processes must fit the culture and your business. The team culture must be matched to your organization's culture. Your recruitment process must match the culture and the business needs . . . and so on. Managing these dependencies well is one of the aspects that separate the brilliant manager from the good manager.

The golden rule

Your own personal behaviour sets the example that your team will follow. There is no way I can overemphasize the importance of this golden rule. It does not matter how well you can talk the talk, what matters is that you can walk the walk. The power of the golden rule comes into its own if you have strong principles on which to base your actions.

Principles and integrity

Management is so much easier if you want to use your power to make things happen. It is also much easier if you have a clear view of right from wrong. If you have a strong foundation on which to base your behaviour, you can behave naturally and, naturally, you will behave consistently. In the chapter on leadership I made the somewhat surprising suggestion that managers should consider faking good behaviour. The reason for this is that from my personal observation I believe that the 'right thing' is nearly always the smart thing. I have seen this approach adopted many times and have come to the view that most people can deduce what the right thing is in most circumstances. The golden rule will ensure that those managers who behave in a principled way will be respected. Your staff will not respect you less, and may even respect you more, if they know that you are using your intellect, rather than your nature, to behave well.

The straight bat

Another example of the application of integrity is to use what I call *the straight bat* approach to tricky management problems. In situations where you are unsure of people's motives or reactions, I recommend that you play the situation from a principled view of trying to do the right thing. There are three great advantages of this approach. First, from my own personal experience, it is as effective, and often more effective, than more sophisticated tactics. Second, it is very easy to defend your actions, and often people will respond to honesty with honesty. Last, if everything goes pear-shaped and you get shot, then you can console yourself with the thought that you tried to do the right thing and that your problems are not the result of playing the politics wrong.

Principles and passion

Managers with strong principles are often very passionate about the things they are trying to achieve. In many circumstances passion is a positive attribute of a manager; for example, it can be a powerful motivator for a team. There is, however, a flip side that the principled, passionate manager must beware of. Passionate people can get emotional in circumstances when the more dispassionate manager can remain cool and detached. There are times when the cool and detached approach is essential: for example, knowing when to cut one's losses, and dealing with your superiors.

Managing the extremes

Managers must accept that they will often have to occupy the extremes of spectrums. The last section described how brilliant managers must utilize, at the appropriate times, both the extremes of passion and detachment. Previous chapters have described how managers may often have to react hard and fast to some situations, whereas other cases will benefit from what I called benign neglect. Almost every area described in this book, from culture to marketing to people management, advises that you consider adopting extreme positions. Managing is not for the faint hearted!

The courage to be ruthless

One of the examples of extremes that may have surprised you is the mixture of kindness and ruthlessness that I recommend in areas such as people management. One of the commonest mistakes I see in otherwise brilliant managers is that they are too kind. It is my view that in many circumstances, kindness inappropriately applied can in reality be unkind, cruel and bad management. Take as an example a seemingly kind decision to keep a long-term underperformer in your team. Someone underperforming is quite likely unhappy, because most people like to do a good job and to be appreciated. That person might well be underperforming because they do not fit into your team or are doing work for which they have little talent. They are a danger to the long-term survival of the team. Others of your staff are likely to suffer increased pressure covering for their lack of performance. All in all, your kindness in this situation may make everyone unhappy, so your kindness may in truth be more to do with lack of courage.

Respect, fair play and courtesy

The word *ruthless* is often associated in people's minds with the phrase *ruthless bastard*. Although I am encouraging you to consider extreme behaviour when appropriate, I also advocate that such extremes of behaviour bring with them a duty to be consistent, fair minded, respectful and courteous. It is again my view that not only is such behaviour right, it is also smart. A courteous request usually achieves more than a curt command. Fair mindedness and consistency will allow ruthless behaviour to be applied appropriately without creating a climate of fear.

Judgement

The sorts of behaviour I am recommending in this book will go a long way to gaining the respect of your staff. There is, however, one aspect of gaining respect that I have not so far mentioned – judgement. To be a good manager you must make lots of good decisions. No matter how principled, courteous and consistent a manager you are, you have got to be good at your job. Good judgement is essential in a good manager; without that I suggest you look for another job where you will do less harm.

Dangers of overworking

I have alluded a number of times to the extreme pressures that most managers work under. There is a great danger that one of your responses to these pressures will be to regularly work very long hours. I have fallen into this trap myself and when I eventually broke out of the long hours habit was able to see that, for me, the effects had been:

- I was so tired that my judgement was very severely impaired;
- I worked very inefficiently and got more work done when I reduced my working hours;
- I made too many mistakes;
- I squeezed out essential activities such as communications and strategy;
- I lost the ability to say no, so did more work and attended more meetings than I should have;
- I set a bad example to my team who started to copy my work patterns;
- I got bad tempered and moody;
- my home life suffered very badly.

If you have got the long hours habit, try an experiment and cut your hours down and see if things improve for you too.

Pareto's Law

The 80:20 rule applies to almost all aspects of a manager's job. Unfortunately it is all too often ignored in setting priorities. One particular trap is to spend too much effort on the new, sexy issues and ignore the boring stuff that pays your salary. Remember to protect your existing customer base; grow your existing product lines; sell to your existing customers first; look after your key staff; and make sure your key staff are deployed on the most important jobs.

Focus, focus and focus

The three most important techniques for making good decisions are focus, focus and focus. In many areas of management you must appreciate that only a few things can be achieved. For example, a product positioning can only include a few competitive differentiators; a business strategy can only achieve a few things in a year; a team culture can only have a few extreme aspects; and you can only win a few battles with your management.

Play to your strengths

A common mistake managers make is to seek to achieve an idealized situation. You have to work with what you have to hand. It is no good you pretending you are good at things you are poor at – better to delegate those tasks to someone with more talent. Organize your team around the staff you actually have. Develop a business strategy that builds on the existing strengths of your current products and services, your current staff's expertise, and your current customer base. Deploy your staff on jobs that play to their talents.

It is no good pretending you are good at things you are poor at

Delegation and micro-management do not mix

Most managers know the importance of delegation, but few managers understand how to delegate properly. Choosing what jobs to delegate, to whom, with an up-front agreement as to the levels of control over the delegated task have been discussed in some detail in previous chapters. The need to allow people to do things differently from yourself and the need to let people learn from their mistakes make delegation one of the hardest tasks a manager will face. You have to avoid micro-management, while remaining in overall control. Unless you trust your staff to work well without detailed supervision, they will never develop the confidence and experience to be worthy of your trust.

Perceptions are the only reality

Marketing people should understand this maxim, but it applies to all your activities. For example, if you are perceived as being unfair then the reality is unimportant; you must always address the perception. Do not make the mistake of blaming anyone except yourself for wrong perceptions. You must listen to your customers, staff, other groups in your organization, suppliers and collaborators so that you know how you, your team and its products and services are perceived. Too many managers are one-way communication devices; you must learn personally, and as a team, to listen.

By default you have created a blame culture

A very common perception that managers find difficult to accept is that their team has a blame culture. This is easier to understand once you accept that you have to go to extreme lengths to avoid creating a blame culture. Are you willing to reward someone who made an honourable failure? Are you willing to allow people to have the responsibility for making decisions and then you accept the blame with your superiors when things go wrong? Are you willing to genuinely praise people who bring you bad news? Can you give constructive criticism with no blame at all? Are you still sure you have not created a blame culture?

This is really important because if you want your team to push their performance to the extremes, to take calculated risks and to embrace change and other challenges, then you have to avoid creating a blame culture.

You have to go to extreme lengths to avoid creating a blame culture

By default your team is regarded as arrogant

Another common perception of a good team is that it is insular and arrogant. Unless you are overtly open and conciliatory to your superiors and other teams in your organization, that is how you will be viewed.

Many of your problems are in your head

You must face the fact that you can do most things that you need to. Your organization, your customers, your staff and the personnel department are not stopping you. If you face the problem, and all the knock-on effects that your decision will produce, then in most cases you will be able to do what you want to.

Value diversity

Sometimes I think that some managers would be happier if all their staff were obedient company clones. To build good teams you need a wide pool of staff with different talents to draw upon. You may need creative people, project managers, good writers, good presenters, good reviewers, analysts, professional workers . . . the list is endless. Each different sort of personality and skill-set brings its own specific problems, and the better the skill, the more extreme the problems tend to be. Good managers should delight in the diversity and excellence of their staff and know that one of their main jobs is to manage the problems that come with any diverse group of talented people.

In any group of talented people you will naturally get interpersonal tensions. It is important that you show that you respect all the different skills and personalities in your team. In this way the golden rule will help you create a culture where people respect each other's talents, even if they do not like each other.

Often you have to give before you can receive

In many areas you will have to take a lead, leaving yourself somewhat exposed. You have to give trust before people have earned that trust. You have to show you trust your team before they will trust you. The same is true of respect; you have to give people respect before they will respect you. Honesty is the same; often you have to behave honestly for an extended period of time before people will treat you with similar honesty.

Humility

I should like to conclude this chapter with a warning about the dangers from your own ego. No one likes to be asked to do something by someone who would not be willing to do that job themselves. In the fast-paced, high-pressured, quick-fire world that many managers inhabit it is all too easy to lose any sense of humility. One extreme view of a manager's role is as a servant of the team. You are there to create an environment in which they can get on and do the real work, such as shielding them from the crap that falls from above, fighting petty bureaucracy and making sure the money keeps rolling in. A little humility never did a manager any harm at all.

Suggested reading

McCormack, Mark H. (2001), *What They Still Don't Teach You at Harvard Business School*: New York, Bantam Books.

A streetwise, and at times cynical, set of business and management techniques from a highly articulate, self-made businessman. I found this a very influential book.

CHAPTER 9

Knowing it, doing it, saying it

I am very aware of the limitations of this book. It's very easy to discuss management in principle – but not always as easy to apply this in the real world. To help bridge the gap between theory and practice here are a number of real-life scenarios complete with discussion of how you might deal with these situations.

Scenario 1

A member of your team who I will call 'A' complains about sexual harassment by a person I will call 'B'

Here is a situation that probably strikes terror into the heart of every manager.

Let's start with what you say to 'A' when the allegation is first made. The important thing here is not to say too much until you have talked to the relevant authorities and done some investigations. On the other hand, if things turn nasty then everthing you did, *and did not,* say may well be used in evidence against you. At the initial meeting I would suggest that you do the following:

- Collect as much information from the complainant as possible. Go somewhere private and try to get all the information you can. Do not be embarrassed about asking specific questions concerning dates, words used, actual physical contact alleged, etc., because such information is key to checking the veracity of the complainant's allegations. In asking specific questions, you need to avoid going into such detail that you might appear to be a voyeur.

- You need to assure the complainant that your organization takes such complaints very seriously indeed and that you will immediately seek advice from your personnel department, and that you will read up the company manual to ensure that the complaint is dealt with properly.
- Ask the complainant if they want you to do anything immediately: you need to check that they are able to cope with the current situation for a few more days as you set the wheels in motion.

I would suggest that you beware of the following:

- While expressing sympathy for the complainant's distress you must not give any indication that you accept that the complaint is justified. You must remember that you owe it to 'B' to accept that they are innocent until proved guilty (I am talking in moral terms here rather than in purely legal terms).
- Do not show any signs of hostility.
- Do not try to talk the complainant out of making their complaint; neither must you be seen to be encouraging them to make a formal complaint.
- Try to avoid promising to do anything specific until you have had the opportunity to talk to your personnel advisers.
- Avoid all physical contact or anything that might *in any way* be misinterpreted as inappropriate behaviour.

Unsurprisingly, the next step is to read the company manual (if you have one) and then alert your personnel staff and seek their advice. Let me make it quite clear, you must do precisely what they say: anything else leaves you personally exposed.

It is difficult to give much more general advice because you will be in the hands of your organization's processes for handling such complaints. There are, however, three areas where I have personally found that the manager can help.

If possible, find out what the complainant wants to be done

This is not as simple as it sounds. Some staff will just want the harassment to stop. Others will feel that they had to make a formal complaint to stop 'B' doing it to anyone else. It may be that 'A' is seeking retribution and wants to see 'B' punished. It may be that 'A' feels that they deserve some form of compensation. Knowing what 'A' wants to happen can have a material effect on the way the organization handles such a complaint, and often organizations fail to discover this crucial piece of information.

Check the complainant can cope with the stress

Many complainants find the process of making a complaint enormously stressful, and you have a duty to ensure that they can cope. It may be that at a later date 'A' will change their view of what they want as an outcome and may want you, or someone else, to confront 'B', with the objective of stopping the alleged harassment. Once the wheels of the formal process have started to grind, it can be very difficult to stop them. If, however, you speak up loudly then you will usually be listened to.

Ensure that the accused person is also treated fairly

Many organizations unintentionally tend to favour the complainant. In the interests of justice, you should be prepared to insist that the person being accused is not assumed to be guilty without there being a strong case proven against them.

Scenario 2

You have been brought in to turn round a failing team and you find the main problem is that a key creative person has left

This is a very difficult problem. Assuming that you are not going to redirect the activities of the team so that the creative role is less important, the steps I would recommend are:

- The first thing to do is to check that there is no one else in the team who has the potential to step into that person's shoes.
- If there is no such person then you need to work out how much you can afford to pay a replacement.
- It can then be worth contacting the person who left and testing out whether they might be willing to return – why had they left? You can tell them that you are now in charge and things are changing. If they are not willing to return, you could ask them if they know anyone who might be interested in their old job.
- It is often more successful to try to offer an opportunity to an up-and-coming talent than to try to recruit someone who has already made their name.
- Find out who in the team has a good network of contacts and use these to approach likely candidates directly.
- Lastly, you can use advertisements and headhunters. I suggest that you include something in advertisements along the lines that creative ability is as important as a long track record, and also include a wide salary range.

Scenario 3

A customer is making unreasonable demands on one of your staff

Obviously you will do everything you can to protect your staff from unreasonable demands, but, in extremis, you will have to decide whether your staff or your customer comes first. However, the cunning manager can usually avoid having to make such a black or white stand:

- You can talk to the staff member and discuss whether there is any way that they can cope with the unreasonable demands. Remember there is nothing wrong with bribery – you can offer time off once the job for the customer is over; you can offer a bonus; and you can offer non-cash inducements.
- You can talk to the customer and cunningly get them to behave more reasonably. For example, 'I am worried that the pressure this work is putting my staff under might prejudice the quality of the job we are doing for you – is there any way we can reduce that pressure?'
- You can rotate your staff through the post that deals with the difficult customer.

If you have to make a choice between your staff and that customer there is no shame in recognizing the power of the customer – an obnoxious but marginal customer makes it much easier to put your staff first. Staff will realize that they may suffer if a key customer account is lost and so may well accept you backing an important, but difficult, customer.

Scenario 4

One of your staff comes to you and says they cannot cope with their work

You should be very grateful that they had the courage to come and tell you. It is important that you handle this in a way that will encourage, rather than discourage, other people to do the same.

There are three likely scenarios:

- First, the person basically has too much to do and has reached the state of the rabbit mesmerized by the oncoming headlights of a car. The obvious solution is to go through the person's workload and prioritize it so they know which items they can drop or transfer to someone else.
- Second, the person cannot do part of their job properly. This might be something as simple as the need for some training, but more likely the person is doing a job for which they have little aptitude. Usually a change of job is the best solution.
- Last, it is a cry for help that relates to something other than the person's work. You will need to probe for the real problem.

Scenario 5

The team has an urgent deadline and people are having to work extremely long hours to try to meet it

There are lots of things you can do to help:

- Even if you are not working on the project then it is worth working long hours yourself, though I would suggest that you do your own work rather than look over the shoulders of the workers.

- You can provide a supportive environment. For example, you can make sure that everyone eats regularly and go to get the food yourself. The boss as the servant of the team is a powerful symbol.
- You can act as support to the project manager. With everyone working flat out it is very easy for the wood to be lost for the trees. You can get everyone together occasionally to check that the work is being done efficiently. You may also be able to use your outside perspective to spot how extra resource could be deployed, and to identify risks that are being missed.
- You can identify when people are too tired to work efficiently and send them home to sleep – by taxi if necessary.
- Perhaps most importantly you need to take a lead if it is clear the deadline is going to be missed and either deliver less on time or negotiate a sensible extension.
- When it's all over don't forget to reward and thank people.

Scenario 6

You have a staff member who works incredibly long hours and refuses to slow down

Ultimately it is an individual's right to set their priorities. If their work patterns are causing them to make too many mistakes or are causing anti-social behaviour such as extreme shortness of temper then you will have to insist that they work less hard, but in most such instances this will not be the case. There are a couple of techniques I have had success with. You can try occasionally coming in late to the office and sending them home. You can try persuading them to take a day off a month – often such people can manage their diaries to block out a complete day to spend with their families.

Scenario 7

There is a major change in office accommodation about to happen

Facetiously I might suggest you reach for a crash helmet! There is almost nothing that arouses stronger passions than changes to office accommodation. The physical working environment is rightly felt by staff to be critical to both their productivity and quality of life. Add to this the less noble feeling of territoriality and status and you have a potentially explosive mixture.

Techniques I have scen work include:

- Find a mother or father figure who is liked and respected by the team and put them in charge. People will tend to behave

A major change in office accommodation is about to happen

much better if such a person is controlling the change. An alternative is for you to take charge and thus put your full authority behind the decisions.

- Make sure that you end up personally with less than attractive real estate. For example, I witnessed my manager lead a team from excellent cellular offices into open plan and by saying that he was going into the open plan himself (and not having a window desk) he kept the full respect of the team.
- Make sure that the principles of accommodation allocation are clearly articulated and rigorously applied. If accommodation is allocated by job requirements, and has no relationship to status, then say so and stick to it.
- Make sure people have plenty of time to get used to the proposed plan. Never jump the allocation on your team at the last minute. It takes time for people to adjust to change.

Scenario 8

A long-term underperformer is moved into your team

A proper, and cunning, move is to ask personnel for their advice on how to handle the person concerned. This will make it easier if you have to get them involved later on.

The first thing I would say is that you should approach the person with an open mind. It is not impossible that someone has been in the wrong job or in the wrong environment.

I would suggest being very precise in your management of the person. Make it clear what is expected of them and try to set realistic, measurable objectives.

If you have concerns with their performance then the $64,000 question is whether you should deal with the issue in exactly the same way as you would with any other staff member. In particular, you will have a clear idea of how much time you would normally allow someone to address problems before you decide you must institute the processes your organization has in place for handling underperformers – *are you any less patient for a persistent underperformer*? I suggest you ask personnel to decide how long you have to give the person to improve.

Scenario 9

A workman comes to you and says he thinks he has drilled into asbestos

There are some issues you cannot afford to take any chances with, and the top of this list is health and safety. Unless you have very strong reasons to believe that the workman is mistaken, you should immediately clear and seal off the affected area. Then you should notify your health and safety people. If you cannot get an instant response you should immediately escalate the issue within the health and safety department, and if this does not yield quick results then escalate it up your management chain.

Scenario 10

You suspect one of your staff is taking kickbacks from a supplier

One of the things you need to understand is when to act on your own responsibility and when to call in the 'experts'. This is one of the cases where you should hotfoot it to your personnel department, which may then refer you to Security or directly to the police. One rule of thumb is that anything that could possibly end up in court should go straight to the experts, whose advice you must follow to the letter.

Scenario 11

The person you are using as your internal personnel officer resigns

If there is an obvious replacement then this is a no-brainer. The problem comes when you have no obvious replacement. Usually it is best to leave the position vacant, covering the role yourself until something turns up. It takes some confidence to leave an intractable problem alone 'until something turns up' – but it is often better than making a bad decision.

Scenario 12

An important project has hit major problems

The first question to ask yourself is whether the project manager needs assistance. If the project manager is one of your top people then you can ask them what help they need and take your lead from them. Otherwise, you may need to take a lead in deciding the strategy for sorting out the problem.

An important role you may have to play is to ensure that appropriately vigorous measures have been taken. As I have mentioned before, it is easy to underestimate how hard and fast you may need to react to a problem.

You may also need to take a high-profile role in handling the customers who are affected by the problem – often you will find that the team involved are more focused on solving the problem than they are on addressing the effects that the problem has on your customers.

Scenario 13

One of your key staff is rubbing other team members up the wrong way

The obvious solution here is the best – you need to explain to both sides how the other side perceives them. Another useful technique is to be visibly annoyed with both sides – statements such as 'I don't care who's right and who's wrong. I don't expect everyone to be friends but I do expect you all to act like professionals' can help to defuse emotion.

It is worth remembering that some level of tension within a team is quite normal, and seldom will it be possible to remove all such tensions – you have to manage them.

Scenario 14

You are told by your management to brief your staff with information that you think is probably untrue

I wanted to include this scenario for two reasons. First, because I do not know what the answer is. Second, because I suspect that there is no right answer. In fact, I suspect there is no good answer.

I moved from being a research scientist to being a manager. One of the things that struck me was that it was much easier to know if I was doing a good job as a research scientist than it was as a manager. As a researcher, I could usually measure in some way how good my work was. The same is not true of management. The world of the manager is often not black and white, it is various shades of grey. In this particular scenario, there are various shades of dark grey. If you toe the party line then you threaten your reputation for honesty. If you admit your doubts then your organization will correctly accuse you of a lack of loyalty. Heads they win, tails you lose.

OK, so what would I do in this situation? I would give the briefing as provided to me, and I would say that I suspect there is more to this than meets the eye, but we will only find out the full picture in time.

Scenario 15

You have a brilliant idea to develop a new business opportunity, but know that if you tell your organization about it they will place so many obstacles in your way that it will probably never happen

I may be about to surprise you, but I know where the corporate obstructionists are coming from. Unfortunately it would be a chapter of another book to explain fully about all the issues involved in developing a new business opportunity; I will, however, illustrate just a few of the issues that are frequently overlooked in developing a new business opportunity.

Is the opportunity scaleable?

I have a colleague who calls this the 'problem of success'. The growth in demand for a service is seldom uniform. If a business opportunity is a success then success usually happens in a short period of time with demand suddenly increasing dramatically. Can you handle such explosive growth in terms of staff, facilities, etc.? You may well need the support of your organization to handle the problems of success.

What is the worst financial scenario that could happen?

Very few managers appreciate the importance of analysing the worst possible scenario if a business opportunity fails to succeed. How much will it cost to manage the small existing customer base of a product or service if you cease to offer that product or service? How much damage to existing products and brands could failure inflict? Could you end up being sued? This is a fine example of why your organization needs to vet potential business opportunities.

Can you protect the opportunity from 'fast followers'?

It is often mistakenly thought that being the first to market is one of the keys to business success. The truth behind this myth is that the first organization to create what the market regards as a leading brand for the product or service often makes the most money. It is not uncommon for one organization to prove that there is a market for a new product or service only to have their early lead overtaken by a so-called fast follower that has an existing brand to leverage, or the resources and infrastructure to rapidly build volume sales and a strong new brand. Many managers do not understand the issues relating to developing a brand and will need to depend on experts within their organization.

I could go on (and on) about all the pitfalls that a manager may not be aware of when developing a new business opportunity. I wish I could reassure you that all the hoops that your organization will make you jump through are really necessary – producing entirely fictional revenue projections is a personal pet hate – but there are usually a lot of sound reasons why your organization will demand to review your plans.

One technique that is worth thinking about is whether you can hide the start of the development of a new business opportunity. It is often possible to find space in your budget to do a bit of speculative development. It can sometimes increase the chances of getting corporate approval for a new opportunity if you can demonstrate some level of prototype. An additional advantage of this approach is that many business opportunities will fail at the earliest stages and it can be useful to weed out the obvious duds before raising the visibility of an opportunity outside your team.

Scenario 16

You have a project manager in your team who has a very laid-back approach to project management and does not seem to worry as much as you would about delivering projects on time and on budget. They have run a number of projects which, despite your worries, have come in on budget and on time. Do you deploy this person on a very important, high-visibility project and, if so, do you institute any additional controls?

I have encountered this situation on a number of occasions. In a previous chapter I said that when you delegate a task, you also delegate the ability to do that task differently from the way you would do it yourself. When I said this I had in mind the fact that the plan chosen to achieve the objective might well be substantially different from the plan you would have created. I think the principle extends to other areas that delegated authority is exercised in a different way from your own. I also think that people have a right to be judged by their results, and if this project manager has a record of delivering then they are entitled to your trust. Having said that, I have found it impossible not to be very diligent in reviewing progress with such people to ensure that I do not lose sleep on their behalf.

Scenario 17

You go to get yourself a coffee and find a group of your team joking about an incident that seriously breaks the health and safety rules

As a general rule I think that managers should not lose their tempers. I also think that you should only criticize staff in private. But there are times when the general rules do not apply. Personally, I think I would do a passable impression of a Titan rocket lifting off the pad. Flaming everyone liberally over such a gross breach of proper behaviour would be entirely appropriate and would show that you do not tolerate your team acting in such a way.

A related scenario . . .

Scenario 18

You come across a situation where it is pretty clear that one member of your team is bullying another member of your team

I would be tempted to publicly tear a strip off the bully, but I think it would be better to give the bully a piece of my mind in private. I would not be at all worried if it was pretty obvious from my body language that I was furious as I marched the bully off for the dressing down. Because the issue reflects so badly on the bully, I think it would be better done in private.

If the scenario was changed to one where I overheard a racist joke, I think on balance it would be better to tear the strip off in public. Telling a racist joke shows an appalling lapse of judgement, but many of the people who might overhear your fury would think, 'There, but for the grace of God, go I'. As a result the humiliation the person suffered from the public telling off would be of a temporary nature. In the bullying situation, you might undermine the person for some considerable time to come.

Scenario 19

Your boss asks you to do something that you think is in your boss's best interests but will harm your organization

There is no simple answer to this question, so I will try to dissect the possible responses you might make and analyze the reasons why you might choose the various responses.

There seem to me to be four possible responses, in varying degrees of forcefulness:

1 You do it without protest.

2 You tell your boss you are uncomfortable with the request and try to engage your boss in a discussion that you hope will lead to the request being withdrawn.

3 You refuse the request, saying politely why you feel it would be inappropriate.

4 You ask your boss's boss, or someone else in authority, what you should do.

How do you choose your response? Unfortunately this is one of those situations that is unlikely to be black or white – it will most likely be an infuriating shade of grey.

One key factor is the seriousness of the damage you might do to your organization if you carry out your boss's orders. If the damage would be pretty minor then a less extreme action can be justified; but if it the damage would be major, or the request is immoral or illegal, then No. 4 is your only acceptable response. Another good question to ask yourself is 'If my boss's boss finds out, how angry would they be that I had not reported the situation to them?'

The second major factor would be the personality of your boss. If they are an autocratic person likely to bear a grudge then I suspect that you would be better off going for either a very weak (No. 1) or a very strong (No. 4) response. If they are usually fairly reasonable then a No. 2 response might well be appropriate. If they are fairly weak and cowardly then a No. 2 or No. 3 could work.

I am sorry I cannot offer more definite advice, but one reason for including this scenario was to show that there will be times when you will find yourself in 'no-win' situations where you have to make a choice from a number of seemingly unattractive options.

Scenario 20

This is a follow-on from Scenario 19. You decide what you are being asked to do is so serious that you tell your boss's boss, who doesn't want to know and says you must make your own decision

I made this a separate scenario because I feel that an important principle is involved. It is my view that if you raise a problem formally with your organization, and that does not work, then you have discharged your responsibilities to the organization. Further escalation can quickly get you a reputation as a troublemaker and can easily damage your career.

Having had no satisfactory resolution of the problem from your boss's boss, I would either carry out the instructions of the boss or refuse. If the issue is solely one of damage to the organization, I would probably just do it. If I were being asked to do something immoral or illegal I would refuse to do it and say politely why. Were the boss to continue to insist then I would ask that the instruction be put in writing – that will usually shut the boss up. If the boss puts it in writing, I would put my refusal in writing and send it to my boss with a copy to the boss's boss. At such times it is very useful to be a member of a trades union and I would certainly contact my TU representative for advice. This would make life very difficult in future dealings with your boss, but there are times when principles must be lived up to, and this is one of them.

Scenario 21

You have a new boss who turns out to be a micro-manager who keeps getting involved in unnecessarily detailed issues

I really wish I could tell you that telling your boss to butt out was the answer. This approach is high risk, and even if your boss takes the message without shooting you they are unlikely to mend their ways. It is possible in time that you will develop a relationship with your boss that will allow you to discuss his tendency to micro-manage. Failing that, or until your relationship has developed, you have to deal with the situation.

You have to realize, and if necessary get your team to realize, that there is very little you can do about it, and try to avoid getting stressed out by something you cannot change.

There are, however, a couple of things you can do to mitigate the damage . . .

First, you should ensure that all the financial aspects of the team and all issues that impact on the bottom line are kept in perfect order. This is one of the best ways to reassure a micro-manager, and provides protection if they start to criticize you – someone who is delivering against their budget seldom gets shot.

Second, make sure you give the boss a monthly written progress report. This will provide both reassurance, by giving the boss extra visibility, and the protection of being able to show that you had highlighted areas of risk in good time.

A related scenario . . .

Scenario 22

You have a new boss who blames you, rather than backs you up, when things go wrong

My advice is virtually identical to that given for the last scenario, with one addition.

Be very conservative in your budgeting, because your boss is not going to back you up if you fail to make an ambitious target. Also be sure not to overdeliver or your boss will inflate your next year's targets. It is fairly easy to push revenue from one year into the next, to bring yourself in closer to budget, and you can then offer a higher budget target yourself next year, knowing that you are already part way to meeting it.

You may want to adopt a similarly conservative approach to deadlines and targets that come up during the year.

Conclusions

You cannot learn management from a book, but you can gain a better understanding of why some things work and why other things can be almost guaranteed to fail. You don't have to implement everything immediately – just try out some new ideas and see if they work for you.

I have only scratched the surface in a number of areas, such as marketing and business planning, and hope you feel motivated to continue reading other books about these topics.

The job of a manager and leader is pretty daunting. This book tries to show how critically important the lower levels of management in an organization are to the financial health of the organization and the well-being of its staff. One of my purposes in writing this book was to give managers greater pride in their jobs. After all, brilliant management is easy to understand but very hard to do.

Good luck!

Index